HOME, SWEET TOKYO

HOME, SWEET TOKYO

Life in a Weird and Wonderful City

RICK KENNEDY

Foreword by
AKIO MORITA

KODANSHA INTERNATIONAL
Tokyo and New York

For Mikie,
who may prefer New York

Illustrations by Akira Odagiri
Cover design by Point & Line

Distributed in the United States by Kodansha International/USA Ltd., 114 Fifth Avenue, New York, New York 10011.

Published by Kodansha International Ltd., 2-2 Otowa 1-chome, Bunkyo-ku, Tokyo 112 and Kodansha International/USA Ltd., 114 Fifth Avenue, New York, New York 10011.

First edition, 1988
Second printing, 1989

ISBN 0-87011-908-7 (U.S.)
ISBN 4-7700-1408-2 (in Japan)
LCC 88-81850

Library of Congress Cataloging-in-Publication Data

Kennedy, Rick.
  Home, sweet Tokyo.

  1. Tokyo (Japan)—Description. 2. Tokyo (Japan)—Social life and customs—1945-. I. Title.
DS896.35.K44 1988   952'.135   88-81850

yet decided what kind of a city it wants to be. In this way, these short pieces are not so much a guide to Tokyo as they are as a guide to what it might be.

Anyway, I enjoyed reading these pieces because they are written in short, clear sentences with wit and style and sympathetic understanding. It seems to me that in Tokyo, Rick Kennedy has found his subject.

Akio Morita

Foreword

Rick Kennedy is in love with Tokyo, and his
thusiasm for what he has called the "sol
wackiness" of the city causes readers of his "T
Toe" column in the *Japan Times* to look at the
with new eyes. He himself looks at the city like a
the angle of his vision is unconventional and
doesn't miss very much (which is especially
markable because the Japanese he speaks is larg
his own invention).

As you read this book, you will discover that Ri
is something of a revolutionary. He is full of sugge
tions on how things might be changed and, curiou
ly, the more outlandish they are the more positi
they seem. I think, for example, that his suggesti
that Japan Railways attach a car with a ramen n
dle counter and a sauna to the last train to le
Shinjuku every evening is wonderfully practical.
the other hand, I am not sure we have to wo
much about an outbreak of a Walkman War, at le
I hope not.

If I were coming to Tokyo as a visitor fi
abroad, I would study Rick's book for clues a
how things are in Tokyo one level below the
vious. Rick can stand on a street corner and
things that only people with a lot of time on t
hands are likely to see. He has written of the T
of his imagination, but also of Tokyo as a city o
mense possibilities, as a world capital which h

Contents

2. Life in Tokyo

3. Fantasies

4. Some Tokyoites

5. The Devil's Language

Introduction

I had always figured a reasonable Life Plan would be first to find a congenial city, then to find a job that would allow me to take up residence there. Sort of in that order.

As soon as I escaped from college I set out to inspect New York, Boston, Dublin, Paris, and Amsterdam, and finally settled on Amsterdam. Amsterdam was about the right size for a city, it seemed to me, and it had lots of nice architecture, comfortable cafes, good bookstores, and an honest citizenry. As an extra bonus it had a funny language halfway between German and English that looked as though it would be fun to learn. So I got a job with an old-line Dutch importing company with a seventeenth-century warehouse and offices on a tree-lined canal in the center of the city and settled in to work through the rest of my Life Plan.

Very soon, I learned that things are not so simple. One morning the boss called me into his office and told me to take a seat. "We would like you to go to Tokyo and set up an office for us there. You will leave in two months. In the meantime, you might try to learn some Japanese, but you should be careful not to get too involved. Many good men have come to grief in the East because they lost their perspective."

I was twenty-six years old. I knew nothing at all about Tokyo. Nobody knew anything about Tokyo.

Back then, there wasn't a book on the Japanese language in any bookstore in Amsterdam.

When I arrived in Tokyo, I was taken aback. There was no architecture. The city was huge—it seemed to dribble on forever. Incredibly, the river was cemented off. The language was intriguing, though: the way to say "I must eat" was "If I don't eat, it won't do," the awkwardness of which suggested that Japanese was not a language of imperatives, and there were *levels* of politeness. In Tokyo I experienced a curiously invigorating sense of foreignness—the opposite of being invisible. The little drinking places I would wander into in the evening, disrupting everything, were wonderful, as provocative as any pub in Dublin, and with distinctly better eatables.

Then one day I met Mikie Yaginuma from Yokohama, just bumped into her on the train, and so much for Life Plans.

As I write this I've spent ten years of my life in Tokyo, more time than I've ever spent in any other city, and I don't really expect to be moving on anytime soon. I'm more a part of Tokyo than I ever was of New York, a city I've always found necessary to keep at a distance in order to preserve equilibrium. (Don't get too involved, would be my advice to anyone contemplating living in New York.)

Even after ten years in Tokyo, a stroll down the street engages me just as much or maybe even *more* than when I first arrived. To me, the Disneyland outside the city is *de trop* because the whole city is one great sprawling Disneyland—a terrific stew of architectural styles, imbued with such crazy energy (in the morning people sprint to catch a train even though they know the next one will be along in ninety seconds), such sublime hedonism (lots of buildings in the Ginza have forty or more cabarets in them, four per floor), such a sweetly innocent passion for gambling (in the pachinko pinball parlors which are on practically every block), and such openhearted congeniality (as in any one of the city's tens of thousands of little drinking establishments).

I have found that if you live in Tokyo as though it were New York, you are bound to be disappointed. You will also be disappointed if you cherish an image of Tokyo as a city of cherry blossoms and shy glances. Tokyo is too busy to have much of a sense of self. There is only one grand boulevard (Omotesando) and the city is in a constant upheaval of wrecking and construction. What is exciting is that large parts of the city are collapsing, and that Tokyo now has the money and the architects and planners to build a completely new city to take the place of the old. Fantastic buildings in a New-Tokyo style are now going up everywhere. We are still refining our subway and train systems. There is serious talk of extending the city out onto a man-made island in the middle of Tokyo Bay.

This little book is a collection of essays about the city I live in which I have been writing for a column called "Tokyo Toe" in the *Japan Times*. Every once in a while someone asks me, "Why Tokyo *Toe*, for heaven's sake?" Ah well, I will tell you. "Toh" is Japanese for "Federal District," like the D.C. in Washington, D.C. Tokyo doesn't have a mayor, you know. It has a governor, like a prefecture. There are islands a hundred miles out in the Pacific which are still administratively Tokyo Toh. So "Tokyo Toh" means everything Tokyo. It's just that foreigners are apt to pronounce it more like "Toe."

I think that if I were Japanese, I would not live in Tokyo. I would seek more exotic climes, like Manhattan or Los Angeles. Undeniably, life abroad is in some crude sense *easier*. Abroad is awash with swimming pools and tennis courts. (To play tennis on a public court in Tokyo, you have to sign up three months in advance.) But I'm *not* Japanese, and a swimming pool has never been part of my Life Plan, so I have found Tokyo, even more than Amsterdam it turns out, an entirely congenial city. My Tokyo is a city of small delights, of unexpected graces that happen so quickly it is easy to miss them, of wonderful weirdnesses, of eerie instances of dedication and an unembarrassed willingness to learn something new, a city that constitutes the center stage of a fanatically energetic nation. Given all that, these pieces have all but written themselves. After all these years, I'm still a traveler in a strange land, a condition which suits me just fine.

Rick Kennedy

1. My City

Home, Sweet Tokyo

A frequent question is "How long have you been in Tokyo?" This is frequently followed by "How long will you stay here?"

Dad blast it, I *live* here. This is my city. It's where I come from.

New York harbors a huge number of people who are not native to anywhere within thousands of miles of the place, but it would occur to no one to ask them how long they've been in New York or how long they intend to stay. In New York you are assumed, unless you spend an inordinate amount of time gawking at skyscrapers, to live more or less in the vicinity, even if the only language you speak is Catalan, even if you dress in the robes of a sheik of Araby. In Tokyo, however, the all-too-automatic assumption is that foreign faces are just passing through.

The result of this tiresome mindset is often eventually to inflict the poor outlander living in Tokyo with what might be called a *crise de residence*. The symptom of this malady is for the stricken to awaken in the middle of the night to inquire in a hoarse rasp, "Well then, where in fact *do* I live?" This can happen even if the sufferer has lived in Tokyo all his life.

In an effort to settle the question of at what point one can in good faith call oneself a resident of Tokyo (a question which must rest equally uneasily in the minds of hoards of Japanese originally from the nether provinces who are now resident in this city), I have devised the following set of guidelines.

You can call Tokyo home if:

—You can push the masses out of the way in order to get off the train without feeling you have created a breach of etiquette.

—When the occasion presents itself, you can sport without qualms a perfectly acceptable *shirankao*.

—You have stopped saying "*Konnichiwa*" to attractive strangers you pass on the street.

—You no longer take visitors from abroad to your neighborhood *sento* for the cultural experience.

—Your daughter has decorated the walls of her room with posters of Japanese pop singers, *and you recognize them*.

—Without consulting a subway map, you know the fastest way to get from Roppongi to Yurakucho.

—You have a favorite barber, who doesn't speak English. Each December, he presents you with a calendar.

—You instinctively anticipate the Japanese holidays but have only a vague recollection of the dates of the more minor holidays of your former country of residence. You have given up full-fledged celebrations of Christmas, the better to husband your energy and resources for Shogatsu.

—Although you are no longer sure you would know how to spend a vacation which stretched on for as long as two weeks, it has occurred to you that it might be pleasant to spend a few days in *Guam*.

—Having learned to recognize most of the *kanji* representing the stations on the Yamanote Line, you have a proprietary interest in the Japanese language. If a foreign friend should suggest that it would be much better for everyone if everything were written in *romaji*, you only smile at the innocence of the remark.

—You have a favorite sumo wrestler.

—You read the translations of *"Tensei Jingo"* in the *Asahi Evening News* from time to time and have begun to appreciate its curiously wooden charm.

—You no longer think that all Japanese children are beautiful.

—You have accumulated several Japanese credit cards.

—You keep nodding to the same people every year at the neighborhood festival, and they keep nodding back.

—You have a small repertoire of distinctive songs for use in *karaoke* emergencies.

—You think Kamakura is a healthy distance away, that Saitama is the country, and that Chiba is on the other side of the moon.

—You are no longer amazed, or even amused, by the mangled language on shopping bags.

—You understand the difference between a Japanese party and a non-Japanese party, and act accordingly.

—You have stopped regarding the skyscrapers on the west side of Shinjuku Station as aberrations, and take a proprietorial delight in the shambles and confusion of the city. You are prepared to argue at length with newcomers that one of the advantages of a city as *organic* as Tokyo is that at least it works.

There are an infinite number of other criteria, but you get the idea. Fundamentally, you can call Tokyo home if it feels like home. Don't let anybody tell you otherwise.

A Most Accommodating City

During my friend Hennessey's first rush-hour brush with the Yamanote Line, I thought he was going to erupt. He told me later that only once before—the night his troop transport was torpedoed—had he experienced similar conditions. He fidgeted frantically all the way from Shinjuku to Gotanda, moving his feet in a spasmodic shuffle to keep his balance and continually rearranging his angular foreign elbows in a search for comfortable niches in the ruckus. When he left the train he continued to twitch, poor fellow.

Not me. I learned long ago that if one simply surrenders, goes limp, becomes as a leaf on the surface of a stream, a ride on a train filled to maximum capacity is comfortable enough. Hemmed in and supported by swaying humanity, one stands with no effort and could quite easily doze off. The secret is: don't struggle. (The rules are different when getting on or off, though: if you don't assert yourself you will never get anywhere.)

At any rate, it is clear that a peak-density ride on the Yamanote Line is one of Tokyo's great formative experiences. All citizens of this city learn from the time they are old enough to stand by themselves, hemmed in and swaying, that resistance doesn't make sense, and the fruits of this lesson are carried over into many other areas of activity. As a result, there is an easiness about social relations in this city, where just about everyone holds accommodation to be a vital modus vivendi rather than, as is often the case in a city like New York, a sign of weakness and vulnerability.

Accommodation in Tokyo is in fact taken to lengths that people who have no experience with the Yamanote Line are apt to find extreme. For example:

Item: Recently, when two of our local gangs decided to stage a ritual shoot-out, they called the police to advise them exactly where and when. The police then cordoned the area off for the duration, informing passers-by that entry was not advisable for reasons of public health. Result: a happy, public-spirited shoot-out with no miscellaneous casualties.

Item: To solve the ticklish problem of JR overstaffing, thousands of railroad men are simply being transferred to other branches of the government, such as the Japan Travel Bureau. Not a great deal of thought is being devoted to exactly how these ex-railroad people will spend their time in their new jobs, as it is felt that good people will always find ways to make themselves useful. In fact, this process of transfer is similar to what happens when Japanese companies take in a new crop of college graduates each April. The new recruits spend their first six months wandering around the premises of their new employer, meeting people and asking questions, trying to find a job that interests them, which the personnel department will in good time formally assign them to.

Item: Every May 1, workers in every industrial concern in Tokyo go on strike. They bind their foreheads with samurai headbands, wave battle flags, and chant ferocious slogans. After an hour, everyone goes back to work, having made their point. It wouldn't do to disrupt company business.

Item: Tokyo breweries have long made it a practice to accept as returns each other's empties. They refill the bottles with their own beer and affix their own labels. It's clearly a waste of time and energy to do otherwise.

Item: The other day I was taking my bicycle out for a spin and as I stopped for a red light the car behind me applied his brakes a tad too late and ran into my rear wheel and collapsed it. Within a couple of minutes a policeman cycled up, ascertained what had happened, asked me how much a new rear wheel would cost, asked the driver of the car to give me that amount of money and, because my bicycle was unridable, to load it in his car and take me home. He did, and when we arrived home my wife invited him in for tea. A week later we received an invitation to his wedding.

There is a wondrous flexibility in a society in which it is more important to work things out than to defend one's arguing space. It allows, for instance, a Kumamoto *geta* manufacturer to switch to manufacturing integrated circuits without suffering an identity crisis.

It calls for practically everything to be decided "case by case," which means, of course, that there are no real rules at all.

It allows for that curious clause toward the end of most Japanese contracts which runs: "In the event of a disagreement both parties agree to discuss the matter and resolve their differences."

It allows official communiques commenting on high-level meetings between the Japanese government and another government to indicate that there has been an "exchange of views," an all-but-meaningless phrase in English, but one which in

Japanese indicates that the basis for accommodation has been laid down.

Tokyo is a city built on the principle of accommodation. That is why the streets wander so.

The Shinjuku Machine

5:14 A.M.—The first train pulls into Shinjuku Station, a Chuo Line local from Mitaka. The doors open and a half dozen drowsy but determined sportsmen stumble out of each car. There are roughly dressed fishermen with their tangle of fishing gear, badge-bespangled caps squashed on their heads; a smattering of sleekly attired golfers lugging bright, new golf bags (they think, "As a golfer, I really should have taken a car"); and two young lads with their bicycles in battered bags. Last off is a stubble-bearded carouser, drifting home from a long night in Kichijoji.

5:21—Three platforms over, the first train from Chiba rumbles in to unload a gaggle of old women from the farms. They are dressed in baggy monpei pants and have huge wicker baskets of vegetables strapped to their backs.

6:00—The ladies staffing the platform kiosks arrive and begin cutting open the bundles of the day's newspapers. Like card sharks at a poker table, they fan the papers out in the racks for easy pickup.

7:45–8:15—Crushhour. Sixteen-car Yamanote Line trains are now roaring into platform 8 every ninety seconds. When the doors open a cascade of commuters spews forth, as beer from a bung-hole. The platform police mechanically urge the formation of orderly lines, but any such artificial geometry is immediately infiltrated by the swirling thousands streaming onto and fighting their way off the platform. It is as if the crowd in a baseball stadium has been let out into an alleyway. One level below, the stand-up noodle stand is dispensing breakfast. Most patrons suck down their ¥250 bowl of noodles in less than a minute, and no one says a word.

9:58—In a tiny, tatami-matted booth at the entrance to Shinjuku Park, the lady who sells admission tickets waits, sipping tea, a curtain drawn down over the window, for the ten o'clock opening hour. She is aware that she already has a customer. He has formed a line of one outside the booth, and passes the time until the park's opening reviewing yesterday's track results in *Nikkan Sports*.

12:45 P.M.—At Babington's Tea Room on the second floor of Isetan Department Store, Mrs. J. Imezu, having just purchased a nice handbag and a new pair of gloves (made in France), orders a pot of Earl Grey and two buttered scones. In the basement, a saleslady in starched apron and headscarf offers samples of pickled eggplant relish.

3:00—A cleaning lady makes her rounds of the public telephones, wiping them off, straightening out the directories, and throwing away the clutter of accumulated notices offering seventy minutes of paradise for ¥12,000. She knows there is a team of three touts following right behind her, replacing the notices, but she pays them no attention.

5:30—In a bright wig dyed pastel pink and green, a glittering cape, and long purple tights, a newsboy weaves his bike through the evening crowd delivering the evening paper. On the sixth floor of Kinokuniya Foreign Books, a young couple put down their backpacks and take from the rack a map labeled "The Japan Alps."

7:00—"Your boyfriend knows that you are a kind person with a good heart. But he is selfish, like a baby is selfish," confides the fortuneteller to the young girl. "Come back next week and I will tell you more." The young girl nods, then goes off to meet a different boyfriend.

9:30—In a cozy eight-stool bar in Golden Gai much frequented by photographers, Mariko passes around copies of the pictures she took during her recent trip to Florida. The general conversation that ensues focuses on how cheap it is to live abroad. A tall young man dressed in a lumberjack shirt runs his hand through his hair. "It's Italy for me," he laughs, "just as soon as my brother gets back from Africa. One of us must stay with our parents."

1:40 A.M.—At Finlando Sauna, the largest sauna in Kabukicho, where management runs a cafeteria for its shifts of masseuses and gives them free passes to movies, Tai Maruyama, a pachinko entrepreneur, sits on a stool under a chilly artificial waterfall. He pretends he is a Zen master, thus putting into perspective the fact that he has missed the last train home. After a massage, he will spend the night here, in a lounge chair. Zen monk on an underground Riviera.

4:00—Only a few bars remain open now. In those that do, the customers all understand each other perfectly, and the mama-sans forgive all. There exists a bond between those who have closed The Spider's Web at four in the morning. They have been to the top of the mountain together, or so it seems.

5:00—The bench sleepers stir at the first light.

The World's Attic

Now that it has more or less sunk in around the world that Tokyo is no longer a city of swaggering samurai and geisha being borne from one assignation to another by *jinrikisha*, a different sort of misapprehension seems to have taken root.

If I am not mistaken, foreigners now generally perceive Tokyo to be a city characterized by bulging trains, hideously expensive hostess bars, and somber office buildings staffed by fanatics in white shirts who work fifteen-hour stretches relieved only by short recesses for calisthenics. In short, a city more or less like any other modern metropolis with a population in the millions.

Perhaps I'm perverse, but the Tokyo I inhabit has a good deal more in common with the Paris of the thirties than the Los Angeles of the eighties. My Tokyo is an antique city.

Oh, I make note of Tokyo's emerging new architecture and I feel the throb of its engines of development, but when I settle into a seat in my favorite art-deco cafe and summon the mustachioed waiter with his hair parted down the middle to ask him for a cafe filtre and one of their chewy *financiers*, an almond cake which has been very popular in France for as long as anyone can remember but which is all but unheard of elsewhere, I feel that I have found my way into a very comfortable, very innocent time warp.

Certain things endure in Tokyo long after they have passed out of fashion in their country of origin.

The young Tokyo blade sports a brass-buttoned blazer with an intricate wire badge, and the lady on his arm wears a ribbon in her hair and carries a parasol against the midday sun. They promenade the avenue, stopping to watch a Sunday painter put the finishing touches on his carefully impressionist cityscape.

Later, they adjourn to a little restaurant in the Bois, where they lunch on madrilène and grilled sole. The table is set as it might have been on the eve of the Crimean War—finger bowls, butter balls, filigreed fish knives—and the wine is served in a decanter with a cut-glass stopper. Over coffee, the lady takes out her fan, for the restaurant is not air-conditioned, and flirts gently as she fans herself. The scene evokes Jane Austen.

Tokyo still has its streetcars, its gas street lamps, its imperial bridges, its ballrooms; and in its cavernous Central Station redcaps are prepared to put your luggage aboard the Shinkansen Express, a train whose exterior design perfectly echoes the famous trains of the thirities.

It is said that the uniforms Japanese students wear are copies of the uniforms Prussian schoolchildren used to wear. These uniforms now exist only in Japan because there are no more Prussian schoolchildren. The leather backpack which the younger Japanese children use, black for boys and red for girls, is called a *randoseru* in Japanese, an approximation of the German *Ranzen*. Years ago German primary-school students used to carry their books this way, but they have long since switched to briefcases.

Calling cards are out of fashion in the West but for a Japanese to leave home without a wallet full of cards would be unthinkable. Most Tokyo tennis clubs still require whites. In Tokyo, a group photograph is a necessary event in every outing, just as it must have been in the West when photography was a novelty. Here, when we visit a friend's house we are likely to present the lady of the house with a bouquet of flowers, an antique gesture but one which shows no sign of being eroded. Our hostess is likely to show us to an antimacassared armchair.

Visit a Tokyo bookseller dealing in English-language books and you will find his shelves lined with volumes of Dickens and Thomas Hardy and Somerset Maugham, authors no longer much on exhibit at bookstores abroad.

The English language itself seems frozen in amber in Japan. While English abroad is bubbling with new expressions and dialectical divisions, in Japan English is taught as though nothing had changed in a hundred years. Japanese textbooks treat English as a language designed primarily for slow, graceful exchanges of earnest opinions and humble supplications. A typical sentence is "We should highly appreciate your kindness if you would send us by return of mail your catalog and price list of fountain pens."

Speaking of fountain pens, in Tokyo one would never suspect, looking at any local stationery store, that writers in some countries have concluded that the fountain pen is outmoded. Here fountain pens are cherished and even collected.

In Tokyo, you can still buy a kewpie doll and a denim shirt. Mickey Mouse and his cohorts will probably continue to amuse in Tokyo long after they have faded into oblivion in Hollywood. Here, there are still chauffeurs, and they still wear white gloves. Here, you can purchase a rack for your toast, and an eyeshade and armbands for use in a poker game, and office clerks still wear sleeve guards. We still use kerosene heaters and hot-water bottles to warm us in winter, and we still use geezers to heat the water for washing.

We still write thank-you notes. We still wear morning coats on formal occasions. We still enjoy gardening and vaudeville and sarsaparilla and the music of a brass band. Modesty is still a virtue here, even in the most modern circles, and we don't like to throw anything away that stands even the slightest chance of being useful later—an antique virtue if there ever was one. Other cities have been swept up and even consumed in the brush fire of fashion, but old Tokyo just lumbers along as though nothing much has happened in the last fifty years except an act of God or two.

There are only two places in the world where alpenhorns are still being made: in a small village in the Swiss Alps, and in Tokyo. I understand that the Swiss are considering giving it up.

Buying a Piece of Tokyo

FIGURING THE OPTIONS

As ex–New Yorkers, our first instinct on moving to Tokyo was to look for what is known in our former hometown as a loft. A loft is a floor of an abandoned factory. Spacious New York lofts are (or used to be) relatively cheap and they tend to be located in neighborhoods with a fair sprinkling of interesting ethnic restaurants and art galleries on their way up.

We thought we could buy a loft in Tokyo and fix it up, thus introducing to the city a new urban strategy. It would, we thought, be just a matter of months before loft living became fashionable in Tokyo.

We look back now and wonder at our naiveté. In Tokyo there are no abandoned factories.

So, we began to look at mansions, which are what Tokyo, without a trace of irony, calls its apartments. We looked at dozens of mansions, but they all seemed to have been designed by the same dedicated miniaturist. In a space as large as a city bus, there would be four or five rooms, counting a bathroom with a midget tub. (We wondered how people living in mansions manage to keep their knees clean.)

Almost never were any of these rooms larger than three yards square, although we did run across a few mansions which, because their developers knew they would be forced to concede a certain awkwardness (a location next to a paint factory, the nearest station only reachable by raft, a three-hour commute on four different trains), had been allotted a whole four-yard-square area for their living room, dining room, and kitchen—their "LDK." But the major problem with mansions was that none of the furniture we had brought with us, which in retrospect seems to have been designed for recumbent giants, could be fitted through the front door.

It would have to be a house then. Surely we would be able to find a house to our liking, perhaps one with finely carved chrysanthemums on the lintels, an expanse of crisp shoji across the front, and maybe a rock garden with a small carp pool.

We put this possibility up to a series of real-estate

touts that we found lost in reverie in their tiny offices, which we learned to identify by the hand-colored floor plans of closets for rent that were posted on the door. "Oh, that kind of house is old," they all said, meaning not worthy of consideration.

At any rate, we were given to understand, these houses were almost never available because developers and their henchmen have discovered that if purchased and demolished, four spic-and-span modern dwellings could be erected in their place.

But these modern houses, the ones so imaginatively photographed with magic lenses and advertised in inserts stuffed into our Sunday papers, these modern houses all seemed to be the product of an inflamed imagination.

It dawned on us that a new style of domestic architecture has taken hold in Tokyo, a style that celebrates bay windows and balconies and gingerbread dormers and Corinthian columns with an enthusiasm worthy of Disney. Between ourselves, we thought of these efforts as the Love-Hotel School. Bemused, we looked at a few of the more sensible houses, the ones that forbore fake chimneys. Inside, the largest room was three yards square and we still couldn't fit the furniture in.

There was, it seemed at this point, one other possibility. We telephoned a manufacturer of prefabricated houses. Three hours later, a salesman called with a briefcase full of plans. We could fit the furniture in, at least.

He told us that his houses were built of slurried limestone, a process developed after nine years of testing financed by a government grant, and that the material was fireproof, dampproof, bugproof and soundproof, but that, no, you couldn't drive a nail into it to hang a picture because it would shatter. So who needs pictures?

A couple of weeks later there came in the mail an invitation to a tour of the slurried limestone estates. We accepted and went early one Sunday morning to Shinjuku to board a tour bus with thirty other couples. On the way to Kawasaki we were shown a thirty-minute video about slurried limestone. This stuff was so good that you could relax in a deck chair with a gin and tonic separated from a raging forest fire by only a six-inch-thick panel of s.l.

We visited a model house in Kawasaki. They would put it up in thirty-six hours for ¥20 million, and it would include fitted carpets, all appliances, a built-in bookcase in the attic, and a whole flock of bushes. We didn't have to take the fake fireplace if we didn't want to.

We had lunch courtesy of the company, then boarded the bus to see an even more splendid model house someplace else, after which we returned to the company offices for tea and cakes and balloons for the kids. At the end of it all we were able to tell them in good faith that we had decided on model 14-C, the one with the wine cellar.

Now all we needed was the land to put the house on.

THE SEARCH FOR LAND

In Tokyo, land isn't so much purchased as passed along. I know a fellow who inherited his family's rice distributorship in Nakano. As his own interests lie more in the line of high tech than rice, he wasn't much concerned about carrying the business on, even though it had been in the family for five generations.

He knocked down the lovely old shop and dismantled the old stone warehouse and built himself a spanking new house on the land. He never considered selling the land, which was worth several million dollars, just as he would never have considered selling the family samurai swords, which he feels he holds in trust for future generations and polishes every Saturday after breakfast with walnut oil. Except in extraordinary circumstances, land in Tokyo is simply not for sale.

Land to build a house on is available at a healthy remove from the twenty-three wards which make up metropolitan Tokyo, however, and it is making the farmers on the outskirts who own it very rich.

But the great majority of this land—mostly rice fields and cabbage patches—is being bought up by huge, multifaceted organizations like Seibu and Tokyu and Mitsui, which level it and install sewers and electricity and their own supermarkets, department stores, rail lines, and bus services, then put up houses of their own design using their own construction crews.

The result is instant suburbs, not very different from the speculative tracts which go up outside any city anywhere in the world flush enough to take a stab at accommodating a burgeoning population.

We began to read *Shukan Jutaku Joho,* the weekly compendium of Tokyo real estate. We learned that the ordinary Tokyo residential plot runs between sixty and one hundred and fifty square yards, that it comes in all shapes—triangular, ellipsoid, patchwork—and that there are great variations on the percentage of the plot one would actually be allowed to build on.

We learned that the ideal plot gets sun from the

south, fronts on a public road (otherwise there is a good chance that the only way you will be able to get to it is via a maze of narrow alleys between neighboring houses), and is located reasonably convenient to stores and the train.

We spent our weekends tracking down likely plots, from Chiba to Misakiguchi, from Kunitachi to Omori. Each weekend we cranked our vision of what was possible down another notch. Each vacant plot we inspected was either flawed in some unthinkable fashion—underneath the Tomei Expressway, downwind from a sausage factory, on the edge of a lake of boiling tar—or so expensive that if we bought it we would have just enough money left over for a down payment on a modestly proportioned tent.

Our friends and colleagues learned that we were looking and whispered advice on strategy and hints on likely locations, adding considerably to the confusion. Cousins and cousins of cousins suggested possible deals. (A developer seemed to be interested in a fallow hillock my wife's sister's husband's brother's wife's family owned in Higashi Totsuka. "Maybe," Aunt Tanaka mused, "if I sold it to the developer I could ask him to sell you a slice at a good price. Of course, this wouldn't be for five years or so. . . .") The mailbox filled with leaflets from agencies which had heard we were looking.

It was at this point that a great truth dawned upon us. The people who were offering us lots all spruced up with plumbing and asphalt driveways were inclined to expect a good deal more money than people who were trying to flog a lot with a dingy house they wanted to vacate on it.

Contrary to ordinary logic, a lot without a house

on it is invariably more expensive than a lot in an established neighborhood with a house of some sort already on it.

This is because in Tokyo houses are written off in just ten years and new houses in new neighborhoods are generally seen to be more attractive, more "modern," than old houses in old neighborhoods. After ten years even the most elaborately constructed dwelling is worth nothing as an investment. It is the land you are buying when you buy a house, only the land.

So we changed our strategy. We now began to look for a piece of land graced with a house as dilapidated as possible. We would tear the house down and in its place construct our own.

With the help of an efficient agent who, once he was convinced that we were serious, hauled us around in his car to inspect three or four possibilities each weekend, we finally, after several more months, zeroed in on a likely spot. It was a good twenty-minute bus ride from the station and the driveway wouldn't accommodate a full-size car, but it was on the side of a hill overlooking a grove of bamboo and I calculated that we could just afford it. We decided to buy it.

I had to have a seal made spelling out my full name in Roman letters—a grotesque thing—so I could affix my mark on the documents of purchase properly.

We went in to the estate agent's office one Saturday and I applied my new seal nineteen times. The next Saturday I had to go back again and apply it thirty-two more times to another sheaf of documents.

A seal expert was called in to examine my work

and after looking carefully at each effort for several minutes, gave his assent. A week later the bank said OK to my request for a loan. We were in! We had bought our piece of Tokyo.

We excitedly called in our manufacturer of prefabricated houses and proudly showed him where we wanted to build our new home. As soon as he saw it his face fell. "That hill, that tiny driveway," he said. "It is impossible for us to build there."

Oops.

DOING IT OURSELVES

Several weeks later, as I was idly turning the pages of a journal called *Japan Architect*, I came across three pages describing a house which had just been erected on a piece of land in Hongo even smaller than ours. The photographs showed a house pleasing to the eye, with a small garden in an inner courtyard. It seemed an ingenious solution to the problem of how to live with circumspection on a small piece of land in an overcrowded city. The architect's name was Yuzuru Tominaga. We went to see him.

Tominaga-sensei looked liked a mad scientist, a man suffused with the joy of creating things. His little office near Korakuen was cluttered with models of fantastic buildings waiting to be commissioned. We told him our requirements (as best we knew them) and as we rambled on he took up a pencil and began to rough out his first idea.

We were surprised and delighted that a man of such talent would take the time to interest himself in our little problem, but we later discovered that there are a good number of fine architects in Tokyo with not enough work, because their potential clients have no land to build on.

(Sometime later I asked Tominaga why he didn't ply his trade abroad or in some other Japanese city where he would naturally attract more business. He told me that for him Tokyo was ideal: few of his clients were much concerned to build in a particular style, so he was free to experiment at working out his own style. Other local architects enjoyed the same freedom—although, of course, everyone had to work within great restraints imposed by space and cost—and gradually, said Tominaga, an identifiable *Tokyo* style was emerging.)

We began to pay periodic visits to Tominaga's office to inspect his drawings, which became more detailed on each visit. We could see cupboards under the stairs, a pleasant roof line, a skylight in the bath, a sliding front door, and great banks of shoji.

We struggled to nail down the financing. Formally, it looked impossible—the mortgage wouldn't be paid off until I was seventy years old (do foreigners live that long, by Japanese actuarial tables?) and I discovered that nowadays one could sign a mortgage committing one's male offspring to keeping up the payments after the torch has been passed, thus making the monthly payments marginally more supportable by taking two generations to pay the mortgage off.

A curious thing: Without any urging on my part, a Get Kennedy His House project team began to coalesce. People I barely knew would greet me encouragingly. My company began to pull strings and bend rules. The outer reaches of my wife's very extended family began to rally around. Everyone knows that building a house in Tokyo is an undertaking fraught with difficulties, so anyone who braves it finds that they can draw on the same reserves of communal support that might flow if, say, they were the community's only competitor in the Olympics.

In time the design was done. Tominaga-sensei introduced me to his designated builders, and one Sunday afternoon we set off—Tominaga, his assistant Miss Nakada, the builder, and Mikie and me—to present ourselves to our neighbors-to-be, to offer them presents (with a business card tucked under the ribbon), and to apologize for the inconvenience to be caused by the breaking up of one house and the putting up of another. It took our little band of supplicants an hour to make the rounds of the five adjacent houses.

A week later the lot was cleared of rubble and the builder gave us a call. He was ready to begin, he said, and would we just pay into his account two-thirds of the agreed-on price so he could purchase materials and organize his work force? Certainly, I said, I'll just notify the bank, which will be happy to advance the money on the loan.

I called the bank the next day. "Ah, Mr. Kennedy, this is difficult. In Japan, banks don't advance money on an agreed-on loan until the house is two-thirds built. How are we to know that you won't take the money and gamble it away on pachinko, ha-ha?"

Shock! We had spent every last yen we had in hand on the land. There was *no way* I could finance the builder for the six months it would take him to get the house two-thirds built. What now?

MY HOUSE, MY MORTGAGE

The longer one lives in Japan, the more apparent it becomes that, although the proper way of doing things is defined with great precision, if for some reason it is inconvenient to do something the proper way, if you are of good faith and are able to draw on the good will of the community, alternate routes are rife.

The morning after we learned of the bank's position, I wistfully informed Tanaka-san, a colleague at the Japanese company where I work who had been following our pilgrimage toward the shrine of a house in Tokyo with paternal interest, that the jig was up. Tanaka-san is wise in the ways of the world and told me not to despair. He went to see Taono-san, our boss, and told him the situation. Ten minutes later Taono-san called me into his office. "I've spoken to the personnel department about the problem," he said. "We'll think of something."

Two days later I had a call from Personnel. "Highly irregular, of course, but under the circumstances the company is prepared to advance you the money you need." We were in! Now we could start to build.

Two weeks later Tominaga-sensei, the architect, called to say that the *jichinsai*, the Shinto ceremony which consecrates the land before it can be built on, would be held the next weekend. Would the family all come and would I bring a couple of bottles of saké plus ¥20,000 in a ceremonial envelope for the priest?

Accordingly, the following Saturday, an auspicious day, Mikie, my wife, and Mie, my daughter, and I went to our little unconsecrated plot of land to rendezvous with Mikie's mother and father, Tominaga-sensei and Miss Nakada, his assistant, the head of the construction company and his father, the two carpenters who were going to build the house, and the Shinto priest.

When we arrived, the priest, dressed in elaborate robes, was setting up an altar, on which he arranged ceremonial rice cakes, bowls of salt, cups of saké, branches of tea leaves, and pyramids of fresh fruit and vegetables. We waited only for Suzuki-san, the head *tobishoku* or construction factotum, who was to bring the four shoots of young bamboo to be placed at the four corners of the altar, without which the ceremony could not proceed.

We waited for an hour. Still no Suzuki. The priest excused himself, saying he had a wedding to attend to and that he would be back later in the afternoon. We sat down to our *bento* lunch and had almost finished when Suzuki-san pulled up with the bamboo. He had gotten lost.

The priest returned around two o'clock and supervised the erection of the bamboo. The ceremony was not long. In turn (me first as head of the house), we clapped our hands, sank briefly into prayer, and shoveled a ritual bit of earth with a ceremonial spade. The priest chanted a long hymn, then gave out a most impressive roar which he later told me was God coming down from heaven. Then I poured saké on each of the four corners of the plot. The land was consecrated.

A month later, when the foundation had been laid, the frame erected, and the roof put on, Tominaga-sensei called to say that we could now proceed with the *jotoshiki* ceremony, to celebrate the putting up of the ridgepoles of a new building, and would I mind preparing the following ceremonial envelopes: ¥10,000 for the head carpenter, ¥5,000 for his assistant, ¥10,000 for the head *tobi* and ¥5,000 for each of his five assistants, and ¥5,000 for the plumber and the electrician. Having briefed ourselves by our book of Japanese etiquette, we also prepared a ¥10,000 envelope for Tominaga-sensei and a ¥5,000 one for his assistant.

The ceremony was held under the eaves of our new house and for the first time we had a sense of its dimensions and situation. It looked wonderful.

We nibbled *otsumami* and drank beer, then drank lots of saké with our bento, all of which was provided by generous and grateful us.

The party went on until dusk, and when we left we had a sense of the personalities of the people who would be building our house. It made the house more real, and imbued it with a character that it otherwise wouldn't have.

We dropped by to see Watanabe-san, the carpenter, several times. Even areas that would not be visible were being finished with great care. Then in February we moved in.

We went to greet our five nearest neighbors, presenting them with packages of soba noodles, symbolic of what we hoped would be a long relationship. The newspapers began to be delivered. The owner of the local saké shop dropped by to welcome us. Up went the TV antenna. The dog punctured the shoji. It was home.

A Mighty Fine Line

People smile when I tell them that I commute to work on the Mekama Line. They are thinking: how quaint. They imagine it must be like commuting by steamboat or Fokker biplane, an antique arrangement which only an eccentric would endure without complaint.

Actually, I wouldn't give it up for anything.

Mekama Line trains are composed of three spinach-green cars built in an age when aluminum was an exotic metal. They look as though they were designed by the same workman-like atelier that designed the armored cars of World War I. Cars of the oldest vintage have a single outsized lamp on the roof of the first car, velvet-covered seats which encourage passengers to sit up straight, and a mahogany-trimmed driver's compartment equipped with brass gauges and enough electrical plumbing to suit a submarine.

The trains operate between Meguro on the Yamanote Line and Kamata in Ota-ku—sort of Tokyo's back stairs. There are fifteen stops, each only a minute or two apart, so the rhythm of the ride approximates that of a lumbering school bus.

The stations are small, sometimes only a wooden platform, and they tend to be decked out with well-regimented beds of pansies and marigolds. Often there is no one in attendance to punch your ticket. Because the stations serve well-defined neighborhoods, everybody on the platform more or less knows each other, and conversations started one day will be continued the next.

If the station is busy enough to warrant a newspaper kiosk, its proprietor will know from years of experience which paper each of his clients prefers and will hand it over without being asked.

No station is large enough to attract the hawkers of kitchen gadgets, the dispensers of packets of tissues advertising the local saloon, or the speechifying politicians who infest the larger stations. Rather, mothers bring the new baby to the station in the morning to wave goodbye to Daddy.

The trainmen on the Mekama Line are a dedicated breed. They see themselves as custodians of one of the last vestiges of a time when Tokyo was a more intimate city. They wear white gloves with their spinach-green uniforms, pull their visor straps down under their chins, and carry their leather briefcases and knitted cushions with them with great dignity when they switch ends of the train. They are as dutiful as lighthouse keepers. When Mekama Line trains pass, the motormen wave to each other.

Aboard the train, passengers nod to their acquaintances before assuming their customary seats. There are fewer announcements than on the bigtime lines—it is assumed that everybody knows where they are going—but when the conductor does address the train he does so as he would address a large, forgetful family—on a rainy day he is likely to bawl out, "Next stop Senzoku. Umbrellas! Umbrellas! Umbrellas!" The posted advertisements are for local concerns like dentists, hairdressers, and teachers of the guitar.

In this way, the Mekama Line trundles trolleylike down the line, linking a string of small villages, brushing by their rosebushes and causing their laundry to flutter.

One hears rumors that the old cars are to be replaced in a few years. That would be the passing of an era, but still the Mekama Line itself will remain in operation as long as people in Nishi Koyama ("West Little Mountain") and Tsunashima ("Rope Island") need a way to get into the city.

Requiem for Golden Gai

To me, and to many others with a congenital aversion to flash, Golden Gai is really what this city is all about. When Golden Gai goes, Tokyo will have lost its heart. The thing of it is, Golden Gai is now seriously threatened.

Golden Gai is an area of a couple of hundred tiny drinking establishments, give or take a couple of dozen, lining a series of narrow alleyways next to Hanazono Jinja in Shinjuku. There is about the bars in Golden Gai a yeasty flavor engendered, it seems to me, by the fact that artificiality and elaborate politesse are barred from the premises. Nobody in Golden Gai ever bellows *"irasshai!"*, and a necktie evokes sympathy.

At one time I thought I would buy a bar in Golden Gai and live over it. By day I could write my novel about Tokyo and in the evening I would slip behind the bar and unwind with an assortment of friends who had in common only a liberal philosophy and an easy interest in the arts. Patrons of my bar, which I would call Rick's, would form a baseball team to challenge the teams of other bars, and we would also form a bilingual improvisational theater group and a string quartet, both of which would be sensationally good. Rick's would have just ten seats.

There are places like my Rick's in Golden Gai now. Sono-san, who is a maker of documentary films by profession, runs his bar called Gu as an avocation. The people who patronize Gu have known each other for years and there's a family feeling about the place. Maeda-san runs Maeda, which must be about the most informal bar in the world. Journalists congregate there to talk, drink the cheapest of cheap Japanese wine, and throw peanut shells on the floor.

There's a bar which caters to comedians, a bar for lovers of hard-boiled detective novels, a bar for fans of the French *chanson*, a bar for flamenco fanciers, a bar for film freaks. You go to one bar and strike up an acquaintance with people who will take you to their other favorite bar, and in this way the whole panoply of Golden Gai unfolds. If you need to know about anything, all you have to do is go to a Golden Gai bar and state your interest: someone will know someone who knows someone who knows.

Golden Gai is a national treasure. Once gone, it can never be recreated.

But now there are plans to build a gigantic new city hall only a short distance away from Golden Gai and the owners of these little places have found that they are suddenly sitting on land worth millions. Although many owners are not at all impressed by money (they wouldn't be running these tiny little places if they were), the prospect of all that loot has caused a speculative fever to rage through these narrow alleys. It can get rough. Some say that fires have been set and people threatened: sell or else.

The owners are holding meetings to decide what

to do. There are "Save Golden Gai" T-shirts and lots of brave talk, but the odds of Golden Gai's surviving much longer than a few years more are not good.

Wouldn't it be an act of extraordinary foresight which would give evidence that the municipal authorities appreciate the qualities which make Tokyo what it is, if the city were to buy Golden Gai from the speculators and designate the area as an historical district?

Japan on $5 and $10 a Day *Revisited*

When I first came to Tokyo in 1963, the year before the Olympics, I was immediately attracted to the city, its bustle and playfulness, and its wondrous cheapness.

At the time, a dollar equaled ¥360. Taxis charged ¥100 to put the flag down and it cost only ¥400 to go from Tokyo Station to Shinjuku, so of course I took a taxi everywhere, just as when I took the train I almost always rode in lonely majesty in the first-class Green Car. An extravagant meal went for ¥1,000, so I ate out all the time, a different restaurant every night.

Although I was being paid what seemed to me only a modest salary by my employer, an old-line Dutch import-export company, I had more money than I could figure out how to spend gracefully, an enviable situation for a young man with no attachments and one which has ever since eluded me.

My three-room all-tatami apartment in the middle

of Roppongi, a quiet suburb where I first stayed, cost ¥15,000 a month, and I remember that I had a habit of breakfasting luxuriously on toast smeared with sparkling fresh *ikura* caviar, a fist-sized plastic bag of which cost ¥50.

I felt a wave of nostalgia for these carefree days as I leafed through an old copy of John Wilcock's *Japan on $5 and $10 a Day*, 1969 edition, the other day.

There is now a spate of English-language guides to our city, some of which, like Judith Connor's *Tokyo City Guide*, are accurate and knowledgeable while others seem just to go through the motions, but in those days Wilcock's book was the only thing to go on.

Wilcock evidently spoke only minimal Japanese, but he loved the city and was committed to poking into every odd corner he could find. He despised the mere tourist, who was for him a shameless creature who lurked forlornly in the lobbies of the international hotels, who bought his gimcrack souvenirs in Ginza arcades, and who lacked all sense of adventure. Wilcock was the first backpacker.

In Wilcock's time, streetcars were still a major means of transportation (fare ¥13), the local public bath cost ¥32, and you could pay for a shot of Suntory whiskey with a ¥100 bill. A good introduction to Tokyo's geography, he advised us, was a ¥30 circuit on the Yamanote Line.

To Wilcock, Shinjuku was "the Greenwich Village of Japan," full of jazz coffeehouses and companionable Turkish baths (¥1,000 to ¥1,200); Asakusa's Kannon Temple was surrounded by ¥100 to ¥150 strip joints; Shibuya was dismissible as only "a sort of minor-league Shinjuku"; and Roppongi, which then as now boasted Nicola's Pizza and The

Hamburger Inn, was the place everyone went to wind the evening down because even then it closed late. Harajuku was boring, a tranquil neighborhood inhabited by rich foreigners.

The Ginza was also distinguished by its array of coffeehouses, which were more elaborate than those of other neighborhoods. Some had ten-piece orchestras, others, like Chopin, were hallowed halls where you could listen to whole Wagnerian operas (some people even brought scores) for the price of a ¥100 cup of coffee (this was before people had managed to stuff their homes with hi-fi equipment), and still others were what are now called "theme" coffeehouses, like Transistor, where all the waitresses were under five feet, or the place where all the (strikingly beautiful) waitresses wore long white wedding dresses.

Wilcock wasn't at all impressed by fancy places, noting sourly that the Okura was "an elegant but rather sterile hotel (minimum $8 per night), whose chief virtue for budget travelers is its tenth-floor Starlight Lounge, from which one can get a reasonably panoramic view of the city. At the semicircular bar, drinks will cost you ¥200–¥400. The hotel's personnel is unbelievably polite."

No, Wilcock was much more at home with hotels and ryokan which fit into his five-buck budget. He put me on to Masuya, the ryokan in Ueno where I stayed for six months in a spacious room looking out on a street lined with willows.

It cost ¥1,000 a day with breakfast, which was so elaborate I had to get up an hour early to eat it. I remember I counted twenty dishes on the table one morning.

My room maid at Masaya, Ume-san ("Miss

Plum"), was a jolly lady thirty years my senior. I learned a lot about living in Japan from Ume-san and she stood in as go-between when I got married. (I was surprised to learn years later that her name wasn't Plum after all—that was only her "work name.") I would surely never have found Masuya without Wilcock.

He turned me on to Fugetsudo in Shinjuku, too, which he describes as "inhabited by innumerable young beats, artists, writers, and students who make their homes there from ten in the morning until ten at night. Walls are lined with avant-garde murals and record album covers and all available corners are occupied by statues, palm trees, or plants, and piles of newspapers and magazines." It was indeed a great place.

Wilcock devoted a chapter to places to eat, and was rhapsodic about the cheapness and snap of chains like Fujiya ("very similar to any good American-type cafeteria") and the German Bakery ("the excellent pea soup with rye bread for ¥180 is a meal in itself").

He was much attracted to the department-store restaurants, because cheap, and he dutifully sought out oddities like Iwashiya, the sardine restaurant, although he was not really at home in Japanese-style places, advising the reader at one point to "sit at the bar and look helpless; you'll be able to point to what you want."

But Wilcock was a great pioneer and the book clearly took a lot of hard work. Still, through it all he enjoyed himself.

He speaks of his communicative strategy at Higashiyama, a basement coffeehouse that seems to have specialized in pretty hostesses: "Your hostess will attempt to make conversation with you but as she won't speak English, this is sometimes difficult. I've found," says Wilcock, "several things to be icebreakers when I can't communicate with hostesses in Japanese: pachinko balls will almost always evoke a delighted cry of recognition, for example, because most hostesses are avid pachinko fanciers; foreign matches or little gadgets or photographs will attract their interest, too. And I always carry a pad of paper with a Pentel pen with which the girls can draw simple things; it's surprising what good artists some of them are if encouraged to doodle."

John Wilcock, intrepid explorer, here's to you, wherever you are!

Mayhew's Tokyo

Henry Mayhew's monumental *London Labour and the London Poor*, published in four volumes in 1861–62, sets forth in great detail the work and living situation of the ordinary people of the London of the time. The captions to the illustrations give the flavor of the book: *The London Costermonger, The Baked Potato Man, The Street Herbalist, The Street-Seller of Nutmeg-Graters, The Street-Seller of Walking Sticks, The Mud-Lark, The Boy Crossing-Sweeper, The Street-Acrobat, The Street-Telescope Exhibitor,* and so forth. It is said that Dickens derived inspiration from Mayhew. Certainly Mayhew paints an unforgettable picture of the London of his time.

I wonder what Mayhew would have made of

Tokyo. I think the wild variety of occupations of the people of Tokyo would have engaged him totally.

Mayhew would certainly make note of the Saodakeya-san, the *Seller of Poles for Hanging Laundry Out On*, who thread their tiny flatbed trucks through the neighborhood alleys while a loudspeaker on the roof of the cab sings out, "Long poles for sale. Fresh green bamboo poles for sale." Only now the poles are not green bamboo, but green plastic.

He'd make note of the Chirigami Kokanya, of course—the men whose business it is to drive from house to house collecting "Old newspapers, old magazines, and any other old paper you don't need" in exchange for a roll or two of toilet paper. Mayhew would marvel at that.

Because we have something of a space problem in this city, a number of jobs are directed at just getting people and things properly stowed. There are Tokyo's famous *Train Shover-Inners*, of course, and the precision *Parkers of Bicycles* hired by the municipalities to jam as many bicycles as possible into the little parking lots adjacent to the stations. There are *Bus Backer-Uppers* who can eyeball the space remaining between back bumper and concrete barrier to the quarter inch and halt the bus with a shriek of a whistle. There are the city's many *Golf-Ball Retrievers* who tend our many enclosed driving ranges. And there are the *Keepers of the Shoes*, those majesterial types who reign over the footwear racks at the entrance of our older restaurants.

Ours is a gambling city, God save us, so we not only have the professional *Bicycle* and *Hydroplane Racers* that Mayhew's London never thought of, but also *Pachipros* (people who play the pachinko machines as a profession) and to serve them we have the *Pachinko-Ball Exchangers* in their tiny cubbyholes, whose job it is to exchange winners' chips for cash.

Ours is an eating city, too, so we have not only a great variety of *Street-Sellers of Noodles, Stews, and Grilled Octopi*, but legions of *Deliverers of Takeout Orders by Bicycle and Motorscooter*. We also have *Bicycle Deliverers of Tiny Bottles of Yogurt Drink*, an exotic calling known only to these parts, as far as I know.

Tokyo's engine of commerce spawns many Mayhew-like jobs: the *Passer-Outer of 'Packets of Tissues*, the industrious *Sticker-Upper in Telephone Booths of Enticements to Assignations*, the *Chindonya Street-Advertising Band*, the *Changer of Posters* (you see them work at a train terminus—a good team of poster-changers can change all the hanging posters in a train in three minutes), and the ubiquitous *Clapper at the Door of Cabarets*, whose noisy invitations are Tokyo's evening Angelus.

Mayhew would also note a particular Tokyo style in jobs which his London must have had, too: the quick-draw flash of the *Tokyo Ticket Puncher*, the incredible stamina of the *Backpack Hauler of Vegetables* from the countryside, the mechanical sweetness of the *Department Store Elevator Operator*, and the wizard change-making dexterity of the *Kiosk Lady*.

Mayhew's London never had *Sellers of Goldfish* at the summer festivals (reputedly a job handled by low-level *yakuza* who have screwed up) or our profusion of *Fortunetellers* and *Street-Sellers of Bubble-Making Machines*. Certainly, Mayhew's London never had men who devoted themselves to the pulling of rickshaws of geisha, a highly paid profession, incidentally.

My Mountain Temple

We live in Hiyoshi, a kind of no man's land between Tokyo and Yokohama. Our streets are narrow and it is so hilly that it seems as if God has played us a little joke, but this has served to stay the hand of developers and much of the area is still agricultural, cabbages mostly. Although we are only twenty minutes from Shibuya, we think of ourselves as living in the country.

People who live in Tokyo vaguely identify themselves with the nearest temple, especially if they live in an older part of town like Nezu or Yanaka where there seems to be a temple on every block. In Tokyo, when the local temple holds a festival in summer and once again on New Year's Eve, the whole neighborhood gathers to celebrate the season, in the summer by dancing, fishing for goldfish in plastic tubs, and eating cotton candy, and in the winter by huddling together around a bonfire while drinking warm saké donated by the temple's benefactors.

In our area, though, the temples no longer seem to be a part of anyone's life. They must have been at one time the focus of the semi-isolated little villages that once made up the area, but now that everyone can get around so easily by car and bus the little temples up in the hills have been passed by. Most of them are unreachable by road.

The temple nearest us is a ten-minute walk straight up into the hills. It can be reached by climbing eighty very steep moss-covered stone steps or, if coming from the other side of the mountain, by following a path which winds through a grove of scraggly bamboo. It is a good-sized temple, whose grounds could (and someday may) accommodate a half dozen tennis courts. There is a smaller auxiliary shrine to one side which has a finely carved lintel and on whose altar someone has left several dusty *kokeshi* dolls, and a storage shed almost as large as the temple itself which is stacked with odd bits of lumber and sheets of corrugated tin, the favored material for repairs. On either side of the temple's entrance is a rampant stone lion, the inside of whose mouth had once been painted a ferocious crimson, now as faded as the color of an antique print. The lions' histrionic pose seems faintly ridiculous, as weeks must go by with no visitor to impress.

After a day's work at home I sometimes wander up to my mountain temple. A visit clears the head wonderfully. It's like entering a quiet, solitary place which has somehow accidentally been disconnected from the everyday world of post offices and apologies and political maneuverings. It is like entering another time, just by stepping into the woods.

Very occasionally on my visits to the temple I come across someone else. They are as surprised to see me as I them. Once last November a bum, with his tattered overcoat drawn close around him, had built a fire and was cooking himself a meal. Once a pair of lovers, who were sitting on the temple's veranda, smiled at me as I walked through, as though we were sharing a secret. And once two young men had spread a thick sheet of plastic on the ground so that while listening to a tape of Michael Jackson they could practice their moves, safe from taunting by parents and siblings.

But most of the time there is nobody at the temple. Visitors come expecting to be alone, in a mood for communing with themselves.

It occurs to me that in my mountain temple, Tokyo, for all its bustle, all its jamming together of humanity, and all its dearth of parks and promenades, offers in its offhand way something that does not exist in London or Paris or New York. Entering a cathedral in a great city for a quiet moment of contemplation is not the same thing as climbing a hill in one's backyard to a craggy old place in the woods, a place which is just a special as one wants to think it.

The Gathering of the Clan

In a world aswirl with change, the Japanese family remains an extraordinarily sturdy institution. It seems unlikely that this is because the Japanese are especially well-endowed with patience or sympathy or flexibility. More probably it's because twice a year every Japanese family comes together to celebrate its consanguinity at an occasion called *ohakamairi*.

Ohakamairi (literally, "visiting the family shrine") occurs at the equinoxes, just as the first flowers bloom in the spring and again just as the heat of the summer has faded. It is a happy, relaxed time with something of the feel of an American Thanksgiving, but with the difference that its whole focus is on the family as a special relationship which has endured over many generations.

I went one recent Sunday and this is what transpired.

After a leisurely breakfast and a nod at the weekend chores, we all piled in the car—me, Mikie, and the two kids—and made our way to Oto-san's house, Oto-san being Mikie's father, the present head of the Yaginuma family.

Although we arrived in midmorning, the house was already a flurry of activity. To get me and the kids out of the way we were instructed to take a bath. Mikie went to the kitchen to help her mother and various sisters and sisters-in-law put the finishing touches on the elaborate meal we were about to consume.

When I emerged from the bath I counted thirty people in the house, of four generations. There was Aunt Suzuki, the masseuse and shamisen player; the two Tanaka brothers—one a jet pilot and the other a jockey—and Uncle Yamazaki, the nuclear physicist and indefatigable amateur magician; brother-in-law Kenichi, the landscape designer and connoisseur of boulders; and his brother Saburo, who drives a truck. There were six kids altogether, including a brand new one, so our ages ran from eighty-four years to one and a half months. Everybody knew everybody, of course. It was as though we had all come home.

The men began to pour each other glasses of beer, sliding soon afterward to whiskey or saké. The women began to drift out of the kitchen to join the men, bearing a procession of platters of food associated with ohakamairi. There were pickles and peanuts and potato chips and *mazegohan* and slices of tomato from the garden and ham and it was too much, too much.

We talked of all that had happened since we last met: Oba-san has taken up tennis, can you imagine, and Yama-chan has bought *another* new car, and Cousin Goro fell off a ladder and broke his arm but they kicked him out of the hospital in two days because he kept getting fresh with the nurses.

One by one everyone drifts over to the family shrine to ring a bell, light a stick of incense, and think back for a moment on those who have gone before, the *senzo*, the ancestors. In the shrine there are flowers and some grapes, an apple and a bowl of rice, and some saké.

In the dimly lit interior I can see inscribed on a scroll the names of members of the family who have "gone across the river." I see my own grandfather's name: Erlon Parker from Thomasville, Maine, who never visited Japan at all, but who is thus acknowledged to be a member of the extended Yaginuma family. On the wall near the shrine is a photograph of Oto-san's mother, the matriarch of the family in everybody's mind, who died twenty-five years ago at age eighty-two. We begin to talk about her and the neighborhood and how it has changed and what she would think if she could see us all.

Finally Oba-san says, "*Jaa, soro soro ohakamairi ni ikimasho ka*"—"I suppose we should be getting on to the temple. . . ." And we pull ourselves together. It takes seven crowded cars to take us all, but as the temple is only ten minutes away, the crush is bearable. On the way we stop at the neighborhood florist, who is doing a land-office business today, for bunches of simple seasonal flowers.

We pick up buckets of water and bamboo ladles and proceed to the family plot. We see many other families en route, all in casual clothes, some with the family dog. It is an outing.

The grave sites are fragrant with fresh flowers. By many gravestones people have left bottles of saké, containers of yogurt, quail eggs, cashew nuts—the favorite food of the deceased.

We go to our plot and by turns ladle some water over the gravestones. To cool them, to wash them.

We spend only twenty minutes or so at the plot. On our way out we stop for a moment at a large plot at the entrance into which have been moved the ashes of all those whose family has died out and so have no one to look after them. Now everybody looks after them.

As we leave, Oto-san looks around at the thirty of us and says, "See how my mother keeps us together." It is true.

Wreck Day

We all labor so intensively over here in the Overseas Sales Planning Department that management, solicitous of our well-being, causes an announcement to be made every Wednesday at 5:30, our nominal quitting time, to the effect that it's no-over-time day and that everyone should knock it off and go home. Nobody pays the slightest attention, of course. We think work is the natural state of existence.

Well, it isn't exactly *work*, in the ordinary sense of the word. Most of the time it's more like batting things around with whoever's handy, if you know what I mean, so don't feel too sorry for us. But it isn't recreation, either, which is an entirely different thing. Recreation is what happens on Rec Day. Foreign companies don't have Rec Days for some reason.

What we do is appoint the youngest guy in the department *kanji*, that is, person in charge of planning and taking care of the details, and we appoint a couple of young ladies new to the department as his assistants. Right, sexist.

The kanji polls everybody to find out whether the majority would like to go to the mountains or the seashore and which season is preferable and if anybody has any far-out ideas. Then he goes out weekends to scout possibilities within the budget created by everybody's chipping in a couple of thousand yen a month plus the company's own contribution, which can be fairly substantial if we've had a good year.

When the kanji has finally decided where we're going, he puts up some posters showing the rambling old country inn and its luxurious baths and the exquisite dishes we'll be served at the opening banquet, just to whet our appetite. Also to make visitors from other departments jealous.

About a week before Rec Day we all get a fat pamphlet from the kanji describing what's going to happen—our room assignments, incredibly detailed maps of everywhere we'll go, contingency schedules, instructions on what to do in case of an earthquake, and a list of what to bring ("extra socks, insurance card, and cookies"). The pamphlet is a bit of planning bravado.

On Rec Day everybody shows up for work in

casual clothes with a knapsack. The kanji passes out bullet train tickets to Atami during the tea break with a plea not to lose them. Just before 5:30, rice balls and pots of tea are passed out just so we won't perish of hunger before we get on the train.

As we gather on the train platform with all the businessmen bound for Osaka we generate a carnival air. Mabuchi-san, a managing director of the company, joins us. He likes to tag along on Rec Days when he gets the chance.

The train ride down is raucous. Beer cans pop and Sugawara passes around a bottle of saké, which we drink out of paper cups. Seats are turned around, legs flung over armrests, and packets of dried squid and other delicacies are passed around. By the time we hit Shin Yokohama the whole car feels like a convention of soccer fans. As we pull into Atami, the kanji warns us that the train stops for only sixty seconds. We make it, just.

At the inn we are greeted by a flutter of maids, who spirit away our shoes and guide us to our rooms, then bring us *oshibori*, tea, and rice crackers. In ten minutes everyone is in *yukata* robe and headed for one of the inn's three baths: the grand Roman bath with its faux-classical sculpture, the rock-strewn bath outside overlooking the bay, or the comfortable old bath of wonderfully smooth *hinoki* wood. You are what you bathe in.

After the bath, we wander from room to room until the maids come to tell us preparations for the banquet are complete and would we please come.

The banquet hall is huge, with a curtain donated by Sapporo Beer drawn across the stage at one end. Twenty-five of us are seated on cushions along one wall, twenty-five along the other, with the division chiefs and Mabuchi-san and three young people new to the department at what would be the head table if there were a table.

The kanji waits until everybody has settled down, then announces, somewhat anti-climactically, that Rec Day has begun. Taono-san, the head of the department, proposes a toast to our enterprise and everyone rushes around madly pouring beer for everyone else.

There's a superabundance of food. The maids keep bringing out dishes, one after the other, with no hint of an end. The curtain is drawn back and a series of skits of increasing silliness are presented.

The first few skits have been rehearsed and feature off-the-wall costumes. In one, the new graduates parade in their school uniforms and an announcer comments as if they were models showing off the latest fashions. Later skits are impromptu, with people joining in as the spirit moves them and returning to their places when their inspiration and energy run out. Eventually Wada performs his famous comic song/samurai chant/dragon dance and everything becomes unravelled.

The banquet ends with a ceremonial clapping of hands—a kind of ritual hip, hip, hurray—and everybody adjourns to *nijikai*, the second round: the incorrigibly jovial to a room fitted with a karaoke machine, where they can warble away to their heart's content, their songs getting more and more sentimental as the evening wears on; others drift off to the mah-jongg room to play doggedly on until five in the morning, with a break every couple of hours for a bath; and the young technocrats to their rooms to plug their Famicon ("family computer," the latest electronic whiz-bang) into the television set and play video games of a fiendish complexity until dawn, to the mild annoyance of Kaneko, who complains the next morning of their little computer beeps all night long.

People straggle in to breakfast the next morning in yukata. Most have managed to fit in three or four baths already, and are thinking about squeezing in one more before checkout. A maid slips Nishimichi, star of several skits who now looks quite celebrated out, a fizzy pick-me-up.

At nine o'clock a plush bus decorated like the Orient Express in blue and gold with velvet curtains and crystal chandeliers pulls up to the inn and off we go to visit a mikan grove, where we pick some to take home, then a short visit to a place famous, the kanji insists, for its smoked fish, where we buy some as presents for those who couldn't come with us, then to a buffet lunch on a magnificent old yacht built in Sweden in 1924 and now a gentle tourist attraction resting at anchor. After lunch a photographer takes our group picture.

We return to Shinagawa on the Orient Express strangely subdued. In truth, we are exhausted. The prospect of work on Monday—quiet, relaxing, soul-enhancing work—is pleasant to contemplate.

"How Long Have You Been in Tokyo?"

After you have been here for a while, you forget how passing strange this question really is. Nobody ever asks anybody, "How long have you been in New York?"

But the question is so ploddingly pro forma that eventually you become inured to it, and each year on the anniversary of your arrival you add a year to the total, as if the resulting figure were one every responsible person should be familiar with in order to fill out a form—a vital statistic. After you have soberly responded to the question over a period of years, you begin to feel as though you are wearing invisible service stripes on your sleeve, like some gnarled top sergeant.

Is the question asked to any real purpose, or is it just an innocent conversation opener? Do we react differently to people who answer, "Oh, we've been here almost a week now and we just *love* it," compared with people who answer, "I've lived in Tokyo for the past thirty years or so—punishment for my sins."?

You *know* we react differently. The response allows us to gauge our relative seniority and indicates at what level of awareness the conversation should proceed. Still, the question is not regularly posed by Old Hands, perhaps because Old Hands have learned that it is an invitation to bores to launch into a history of their involvement with the Orient ("Well, let's see, I came to Tokyo for the first time in 1952, by way of Bangkok, actually . . ."), but when Old Hands do ask it their tacit meaning is, "Are you one of us?"

Of course, when you learn how long somebody has been here and apply the appropriate calculus, you can devine something about their capacity to pursue a disciplined course of action without being unduly distracted, a particularly admirable trait in a city as potentially distracting as Tokyo. If a young lady should tell you, for example, that while she arrived in Tokyo from the School of Extreme-Orient Studies at the Sorbonne just last spring, she is enjoying her job as cultural-affairs commentator on NHK television immensely and that she is amused to see how a well-known theatrical group is rehearsing the light satirical play she dashed off for them (in Japanese, it goes without saying), it is polite to indicate that you are impressed. Such brazen one-upmanship is not easily parried.

On the other hand, you can determine something about a person's capacity for sympathetic interaction with another culture if they tell you they have lived in Nishi Azabu since before it was called that, and that, sure, they can get along more or less in the lingo—enough anyway to keep the taxi driver going in the right direction—but that really nobody in their right mind can expect to come to grips with the language in less than a lifetime—they've got *three different alphabets* for God's sake!

Sometimes a Japanese you have just been introduced to will inquire in a conversational first serve, "How long have you . . .?" In this case, the motive is obviously not to gauge relative seniority. It is only a sort of salutation in interrogative form. A good way to respond to the question from a Japanese, at the risk of short-circuiting the conversation, is to ask your interlocutor, "How long have *you* been in Japan?" The flat-footedness of the question becomes immediately apparent.

Another all-too-familiar and equally problematical question is, "Where are you from?" If you say, "Yokohama," the next question is sure to be, "No, I mean *really*," suggesting that somehow Japan's second city is only as real as Oz. The only acceptable response seems to be some easily recognizable place name like New York or California or Paris, even if you have never lived in any of these places long enough to fall in and out of love.

I suppose people who insist on settling down in a different country from the one they happen to have been born in just have to learn to live with this sort of question, at least until the world's population becomes sufficiently shuffled that the question is patently no longer meaningful.

This Cozy Country

So *Esquire* columnist Bob Greene comes to Tokyo and freaks out—all this bowing, people so energetic, naked ladies and Miami Vice in Japanese on TV— and goes home exhausted, suffering from cultural concussion.

It works the other way, too, of course. A Japanese engineer I work with, a sophisticated guy who has just figured out a way to record the entire Library of Congress on a single compact disc, comes to me and says he has been invited to give a ten-minute presentation of his work at Bell Labs in New Jersey and he wants to know *how to greet them*.

Ours has to be the last generation which clutches when it travels to the other side of the world.

It must be less traumatic for foreigners to come to Japan, though, than for Japanese to venture abroad. Japan is so cozy, and abroad is so, well, *brusque*.

Think of it this way: Japanese go to New York and immediately get yelled at for not closing the taxi door, then they get looked at strangely for waiting for the green light before crossing the street. They conclude that New York is the frontier.

All sorts of functionaries make it plain that they expect to be tipped (even for opening the door of a taxi), but they rarely seem satisfied with the amount they are given. Purchases are hardly wrapped and nobody seems much concerned about being thought of as polite.

Leafing through the magazines at a New York newsstand (which they soon learn they are not encouraged to do), Japanese travelers discover that American cars have names like Matador and Cobra and that advertisements for them snarl about horsepower and brakes. They recall wistfully that Japanese cars have names like "Parsley" and "Ballade" and that advertisements for them show young people holding hands.

In New York the buildings are monstrous, closing out the sky, while the open spaces of America extend to an empty horizon. Japanese think of the landscape of both urban and rural America as bleak, lonely, uncomfortably majestic. In Japan, there is no "Marlboro Country" which demands to be lived up to (Golden Bat Country, maybe), and in Tokyo there are no boulevards scaled to make the stroller feel insignificant. All Tokyo is a jumble, like the family living room on a lazy Sunday afternoon.

Japanese go to the States and see television news programs featuring anchor people (tough, rugged nomenclature, that) who speak with *enormous* confidence and *tremendous* vigor. In Tokyo, TV is more low key, as if it were put on by the neighborhood amateur dramatic society or a bunch of friends in a silly mood.

American sports on TV seem to celebrate aggression—the slow-motion playbacks seldom analyze form, but keep focusing in on people getting hammered. Favorite sports on Japanese TV are high-school baseball tournaments, marathons through the middle of large cities while the citizenry waves little paper flags as encouragement, and sumo, which although certainly violent (for several seconds at a time) is so drenched in ritual and weighed down by the roly-poly physiques of its participants that it just serves to underline the singularity of an act of violence.

In America, few people seem to have a hometown to return to. Everybody has to pump their own gas. Drunks are hauled off to jail. Children are scolded. People write angry things in funny letters on the sides of buildings. Handshakes are wrestling matches. It is difficult to spell people's names and they never give you their card. A party means standing holding a strong drink while trying to make conversation with a lot of people you don't know. People are surprised when a train is on time.

Japan, on the other hand, is a country where children are carried warm and snug on their mother's back, pampered with cute little toys (the Japanese cute little toy industry is big business), and sung the sweetest nursery songs in the world. When they reach kindergarten, Japan Railways, like a proud father, hangs their watercolors in the stations.

The Japanese grow up accustomed to being fussed over and as adults the habit lingers. In Japan, as the evening approaches the shutters of the house are pulled shut and after a hot bath drawn up to the chin and a dinner prepared by the loving lady of the house, the family arranges itself around the *kotatsu* to sip sweet juices or warmed saké. (Japan must be the only country whose national beverage is coddled.) After an hour or two of easy conversation—no rapier witticisms or thundering arguments are allowed—the family finishes off with bowls of *ochazuke*, rice pablum, a dish which puts few demands on the digestive system, then rolls into beds laid out inches away from each other which cannot be fallen out of. Rabbit hutches, by definition, are cozy.

In the morning, the Japanese are swept off to work on a tide of fellow commuters. The train is crowded, as the womb is crowded, but there is no cause for anxiety because each stop is carefully announced (perhaps in extraordinarily dulcet recorded tones) and everyone is informed which side the doors will open on, told to hang on tight as the train approaches a corner, and reminded not to forget their umbrellas. It is like being taken to school by one's mother.

In Japan, the whole country is one great commune. Almost everyone describes themselves as "middle class," so there is little of the gnawing pressure to improve oneself that drives Americans. There's a single time zone and only one language, which most Japanese feel is their own secret language. The country's schoolchildren all study the same textbooks to the same schedule. To venture forth from Japan is for a Japanese like leaving the bed for a blizzard.

The Japanese police are avuncular to the point of being prepared to lend carfare. They take kids aside for walking sloppily or riding their bicycle in a reckless manner, and they make it their business to know when a baby is born on their beat. The Tokyo subways put up artful posters reminding people not to get their fingers caught in the closing doors and to surrender their seats to their elders.

At stoplights Japanese drivers switch off their high beams so as not to dazzle the driver in front. A phone call brings bowls of noodles to any house, even in a downpour. A child crossing the street holding a yellow flag could stop an army. Visitors to the house, even the paperboy on a collection run, bring a little gift. When you join almost any Japanese organization, you can expect a welcoming party in your honor. The whole country saves old newspapers.

Youngsters who want to be thought of as malcontents cut their hair bebop style and wear black nylon jackets which say something like BAD SOLDIER TEAM WORLD WAR ESTABLISHED 1987 across the back. Japanese painters of a romantic inclination have to move to Paris because in Tokyo there is no *Sturm* or *Drang*.

When American students from the American School who have grown up in Japan go abroad to experience their homeland, they come back reeling. Life in Tokyo is a snuggle; life abroad is a hockey game.

Can foreigners resident in Japan partake of this coziness? Absolutely, but they should be wary. It is addictive.

2. Life in Tokyo

The Advanced Rules

After a week or two you pretty well know the basic rules—take off your shoes before entering a house, don't use soap in the bathtub, don't try to close the door of the taxi, be polite, don't argue, don't jaywalk. But there is a more advanced set of rules, a more subtle protocol, which only becomes apparent after some time has passed. In an effort to shorten the time required for outlanders to adapt to the routine in our great city, I list below some of these more advanced rules:

1. It is considered bizarre to count your change.

2. Men should be prepared to spend at least forty minutes in the barber chair. To tell the barber that all you want is a quick trim is to insult a craftsman.

3. It is not allowed to stroll carelessly in the rain without an umbrella. If you should whistle a tune while strolling in the rain you will arouse even greater suspicion. *Singing* in the rain is cause for committal.

4. Avoid making a great show of pleasure when you wipe your face with an *oshibori*. Take this little pleasure in stride.

5. Don't bow too deeply or too solemnly. Do it with a sense of humor, as if to say "Look what strange things custom demands of foreigners."

6. Don't drive a dirty automobile. Don't ride a clean bicycle.

7. In the entranceway, learn to jam your feet quickly into your shoes. Putting on your footgear

carefully and lacing them up keeps everybody waiting.

8. In the office, a sure way to get a reputation as a person of independent and unpredictable ways is to put your feet on the desk.

9. Don't broadcast your interest in the Japanese arts too loudly. You risk embarrassing people who have never been to a Kabuki performance or a tea ceremony. And you should realize that an enthusiasm for the intricacies of *kanji* is roughly equivalent to a burning interest in spelling.

10. Never turn down a casual invitation to go drinking with Japanese colleagues. It is not a casual invitation.

11. When someone pours you a beer, raise your glass or at the very least touch the glass while the beer is being poured.

12. Never end a telephone conversation just by saying goodbye and hanging up. Utter a ten-second litany of polite phrases in a gradual decrescendo and only then, most reluctantly, replace the receiver.

13. Do not be afraid of silences during a conversation. People who are able to be silent with each other are friends.

14. Never say no. If pressed, cock your head and say "Ahhh—" It amounts to the same thing. But you knew that.

15. The trains have their own set of rules. Such as:

   a. Don't give up your seat to a woman unless she is obviously infirm. (She will only give it to a kid.) If someone should vacate the seat you are standing before, wait a beat or two before slipping into it: we're all civilized here.

   b. Before you take a seat, remove your possessions

from the overhead rack so that you can keep them on your lap.

c. When a train with an acquaintance on it is pulling out of the station, continue to wave goodbye until the train is out of sight.

d. When the train pulls into the station, let people getting off push you out of the way. Do not attempt to make way for them. Also, don't stroll hands-in-pockets in a crowded station. Scurry, or you will impede traffic.

Levels of Perception

It is curious that foreigners' first impressions of Tokyo (accumulated after, say, seven days in the city), second impressions (after maybe seven months), and third impressions (after seven years) follow a predictable pattern. For example:

First impression: Good grief these trains are crowded! How do they bear it?
Second impression: They bear it.
Third impression: Crowded?

1. People are so diligent. They love to work.
2. They're not working *hard*.
3. What you have to understand is, Japanese work is one thing and Western work is another.

1. The Japanese educational system is superb.
2. The Japanese educational system is rotten.
3. The Japanese educational system is what makes the Japanese Japanese.

1. *Kanji* are very interesting.

2. Kanji are an invention of the devil.
3. Kanji are kanji.

1. The Japanese have no sense of humor.
2. The Japanese have a *Japanese* sense of humor.
3. What's so funny?

1. Have you noticed, Japanese children are so beautiful.
2. Japanese children are overindulged little monsters.
3. Poor little beggars, the nail that protrudes will be hammered down.

1. Japanese addresses are useless.
2. Oh, with a few lucky inquiries and a bit of patience you can eventually find almost any place.
3. Addresses are a Western hang-up.

1. In Japan, everybody studies English but few can speak it.
2. They know more English than they let on.
3. It isn't English.

1. Soba is such a refreshing quick snack, and so *Japanese*!
2. Soba is boring.
3. So what?

1. People are very generous. They give presents with the slightest excuse.
2. It's a bother to have to give presents all the time.
3. The secret of gift giving is artful recirculation.

1. Jeez, did you feel that? The whole building shook!

2. Was that a tremor just now?
3. Please pass the marmalade.

The Urban Imagination

Akira Muramatsu rose at dawn, pulled on a favorite sweater, packed the lunch his wife had made him the night before in his creel, and cycled down to the station to catch an early train to his favorite fishing grounds. When he arrived just after seven, there were already a dozen men seated around the cement pool adjacent to Ichigaya Station, and by eight all of the beer-crate seats around the pool had been taken.

All day long, the fishermen languorously dangled their lines in the pool, oblivious of the rumbling of the trains and the city all around them, each of them dreaming of a faraway province where soft breezes stir a grove of pines and the only sound is the crickets and the gurgle of the stream. Far, far away. Far away from Ichigaya.

Tokyo seems a city where reality has teeth, where there is no escape from the cacophony, the confusion, the incipient chaos of a metropolis whose throttle is jammed wide open. But for those who can imagine, there are many escapes.

In the late afternoon Akira Muramatsu returned home and offered up to his wife the small trout and the medium-sized mackerel he had caught. He then adjourned to the local public bath, where as he soaked in the communal tub he gazed up at a huge mural of Mount Fuji. With no effort at all, he imagined himself to be in the bath of a rustic country inn in Hakone looking up at the real Mount Fuji through the evening mist on Lake Ashinoko.

Young Tokyoites, having been brought up to think of themselves as budding samurai during the Boys' Festival or attendants at the royal court during the Dolls' Festival, find it easy to transport themselves to the Le Mans circuit behind the wheel of a Ferrari by simply dropping ¥100 into the slot of a video game. In the same way they go on bombing runs, play world-class tennis before cheering crowds, and battle teams of knife-throwing guardians of the Treasure Room. They explore these other worlds for hours at a time, their faces rapt with concentration. They have escaped.

It doesn't cost much to escape to the fairway of a famous golf course, either. For the price of a mug of beer, you can spend thirty minutes at the ninth hole of Augusta, with the wind at your back and fifty balls in a pail at your ankle. In the middle of the city you can go skiing. The slope is plastic, but it is only a trick of the mind to imagine yourself in Vail.

Tokyo's love life is lusher than anything in even the most extravagantly lurid movie, because no movie would risk ridicule by using one of our fantastic love hotels as a set. For Tokyoites, though, the love hotel is a fantasy as ordinary (and as full of expectations) as the morning post.

In the evening I can take you to a country inn with a dirt floor and tables worn smooth with age, where all the waitresses speak with a Tohoku lilt. It is on the fifth floor of a building in the Ginza, but surely it is also in Aomori. In the Ginza there is also a replica of a turn-of-the-century Parisian bistro, which is more perfect than anything in Paris itself because it is absolutely unembarrassed in its duplicity. We could visit both these places the same evening, telescoping both time and geography, then I could invite you home for a cup of tea while we gaze out on the vast landscaped garden behind my house. If you tell me that my garden is only as large as a billiard table I will tell you that this is only a matter of perspective, for in my mind it covers acres.

The interior tableaux of the people of Tokyo are as real and rich in detail as a medieval tapestry.

Stat Madness

Every evening a platoon of pollsters armed with clipboards and earnest expressions takes up position outside Shibuya Station to engage the scurrying hordes with the question of the day: "Excuse me. Just a moment of your time. Do you worry that your children only study and hardly play at all?" "Have you ever rented a video cassette from a vending machine?" "Would you welcome a foreigner into your home?"

Tokyoites are old hands at responding to questionnaires. We like it, even puffing up a little, when we are picked out of the crowd to answer for Everyman. We imagine that our compiled responses will be useful in helping us to gauge how average we are; in determining what percentage of us feel despondent, happy, extremely happy; in discerning what the older generation really feels about the younger; in finding out if we are handling our money as prudently as the neighbors. Polls model the national character.

The local media are awash with statistics about every detail of our lives, solemnly charting the erratic course of our civilization as it caroms from week to week. People seem to feel that if they have a good count of how many times an event has taken place, then in some mysterious way they have an insight into the cause of the event, and perhaps even some control over it. It is the final justification for social science.

Japan's English-language press is particularly enamored of statistics. Here are some actual examples of our statmania, as culled from the newspapers of the last couple of months:

"Twenty-seven died from eating *mochi* (sticky rice cakes) when it stuck in their throat on the first two days of the new year. Last year only twenty-one people died from eating mochi."

"The National Police Agency reports 70.5 million people visited Shinto shrines and Buddhist temples during the first three days of 1986, down by 2.25 million from the previous year and the lowest turnout in four years."

"A survey by the Dai-Ichi Kangyo Bank reports that children this year were given an average of ¥22,793 as New Year gifts from an average of 7.7 persons, up ¥1,731 from last year."

"This year about 11 million business cards were exchanged daily in Japan, up about 6 percent from last year."

"Companies spent ¥3.62 trillion on entertainment expenses across the country last year, hitting a new record, according to the National Tax Administration Agency. The previous high was ¥3.523 trillion spent the year before last."

"Thirty-six percent of salaried men actively go out to drink with fellow workers three to five times a month. Thirty-two percent go out once or twice and 16.2 percent go out six to eight times; 7.1 percent of salaried men never join."

"The monthly number of workdays last year decreased by 0.1 day to 21.8 days, as compared with the year before, while overtime increased 1.5 percent."

"Ninety percent of youth are content with life, up 33 percent since 1970, according to the Management and Coordination Agency."

"A government survey found 39.7 percent of Japanese believe Japan is moving in the right direction, the highest figure in seven years. Those saying Japan is taking a wrong course dropped from 26.8 percent to 25.5 percent."

"One out of four elementary school pupils and one out of every two junior high school students attend cram schools. Those percentages are much higher than those reported in 1976 by the Ministry of Education. Of the cram school operators, 36.8 percent said their business pays well; 32.5 percent said that it pays so-so; 14 percent said it is difficult to make a profit and 2.7 percent said it is very difficult."

"The Prime Minister's Office released a survey saying 90 percent of the people are afflicted by noise and vibration from trucks and other vehicles, but that only 20 percent of those have complained, up 16 percent from the previous survey two years ago."

"The average length of a baseball game has surpassed three hours in the past ten years, a gain of thirty-eight minutes, in sharp contrast to the less than two hours a game took until 1961."

"Boys' comics have a single stereotype of women.

While girls in the girls' comics have a variety of hairstyles—long hair (55 percent), short hair (31 percent), semi-long hair (10 percent)—89 percent of the heroines in boys' comics are longhaired."

"The Hakuhodo Institute of Life and Living reports that, when people were asked 'What is exciting in your world?', responses were as follows:

Tokyo Disneyland	50.8 %
Jazz dancing	47.4
Homemade cookies	45.1
West Coast of U.S.A.	44.0
Personal computers	42.3
Four-wheel-drive cars	39.4
Azabu	38.6
BMW and Mercedes Benz	36.2
Central heating	35.8."

"According to the National Police Agency, sex-related businesses throughout the country totaled 16,781 as of last October, representing a drop of 897 since the New Law to Control Business Affecting the Public Morals went into effect. Love hotels were down 6.6 percent; 'adult shops'—which sell pornographic magazines and sex gadgets, both serious and joking—decreased by 12.6 percent. Confusing the picture, however, were striptease joints, which were said to have increased by 13.7 percent, and massage parlors, which increased by an extraordinary 38.2 percent."

"In 1976 there were 1,490,000 digits in the national timetable of the Japan Railways. This year there were 1,950,000 digits."

"All information provided in Japan through media, communication networks, publications, and school rooms in the year ending last March amounted to 255,000 trillion words, a rise of 7.4 percent over the previous year."

This way lies madness.

The Terrible Cultural Burden of Working Late

There is a feeling, I know, that the world economy would be better aligned if only the Japanese wouldn't work so hard. People who keep track of such things say the average Japanese worker puts in four hundred more hours each year than the average worker of the next longest laboring country, West Germany. By my reckoning, this would make the Japanese year two months longer than the German year. Adding further to this disgraceful piling up of working hours, ticking like time on a taxi meter, is the Japanese attitude toward vacations: the world seems to think that for a Japanese to succumb to a vacation is for him akin to being pulled out of the big game by a coach who feels he needs a little rest.

Even so perceptive an observer as James Fallows recently wrote in *The Atlantic* that the Japanese work so hard because it is in their genes, or something. They don't know how not to work, he suggested.

I am afraid this is nonsense. What has happened is that the Japanese have latched onto the idea that willingness to work overtime is a measure of dedication to the job and loyalty to the company, even a measure of one's intrinsic worth as a human being, and now they are stuck with it. The idea is as uncomfortably mechanical as the imperative to have sex every evening or risk being thought of as being sadly deficient in *élan vital*.

As a result, when the quitting bell sounds in my company at 5:30, nobody moves. Even to give the bell notice is thought somehow to be a sign of selfish preoccupation. At 7:00, most people are still at their desks, although very little *if any* extra work has been done. The only difference is that there is now a certain relaxed jocularity, a more pronounced "we are all in this together" feeling. Clearly, overtime is a habit. People have built it into their lives, so that now a Japanese husband returning home early (that is, before his children have gone to bed) *slinks* into the house so as not to be noticed by the neighbors. All this is not to say that anybody *enjoys* hanging around the office hours after quitting time.

Because overtime is so endemic, it is taken for granted. Thus, people who leave work at the official quitting time opt themselves out of the real action. Because the Japanese decision-making process is so stately—slam-bang decisions are very bad style—the prime decision-making time is after hours. A decision come to or an idea broached late at night, when the unserious people have faded away, is somehow more authentic. Everyone who realizes this, of course, is trapped by their realization into a regime of hanging around late into the night *just in case* somebody in the office should have the energy to moot an idea.

Actually, for the sake of international equanimity, it is probably best that the Japanese work force continue to doggedly put in these (mostly unproductive) hours after normal quitting time. Think of the consequences if everyone came to work in the morning fresh, their creative batteries recharged, knowing they had only eight hours in which to get the job done!

It Will Never Happen

In this city things tend to be done in prescribed ways, partly because in an extremely crowded urban environment gratuitous deviation can result in system breakdown and partly because winsome variation for its own sake has never been in fashion. For instance, it will never happen that:

—A pachinko parlor plays Vivaldi for background music.

—The Emperor gives the V sign to the crowd.

—A politician orating at a train station is heckled by commuters.

—An engine driver pulls out of the station with his elbow on the sill.

—A newspaper delivery boy lofts a paper onto a subscriber's stoop.

—The crowd at the ballgame is pensive.

—The teen-age cutie on TV is a glorious soprano.

—The last train is empty.

—In a face-off, a sumo wrestler cracks a grin.

—The *bosozoku* motorcycle gang gathers for a late-evening potluck supper.

—After a terrible performance at the theater, someone boos.

—At the Monday morning *chorei* meeting, nobody has anything in particular to say and the meeting adjourns in ninety seconds.

—An *aizuchi* lady disagrees.

—A barber gives a trim in less than thirty minutes.

—A businessman takes off his jacket to reveal a resplendent pair of suspenders.

—At the neighborhood Bon dance, a brief flurry of the Charleston.

—The policeman at the *koban* admits he has no idea where that address scribbled on the back of an envelope is.

—Two old ladies in kimono passing in the street each bow *only once*.

—As the train pulls into the station, the conductor announces "Hey, hey, hey—Shibuya, folks!"

—In a Ginza department store, a customer picks out a tie but cannot find a salesperson to take his money.

—Heard issuing from a *karaoke* bar: Schubert lieder.

—Office workers spend an hour over their *donburi* lunch discussing the affairs of the day.

—One week, all three hundred weekly magazines have the same cover girl. Nobody notices.

—The street solicitors for Cambodian orphans announce that they have met their goal.

—Sotheby's has an auction and no one from Japan buys anything.

—The company president's limo is brown.

—At five o'clock the bell rings and everybody goes home.

Won't happen, but one can always hope.

The Sounds of Tokyo

It was drizzling, and as I had no umbrella I waited at the top of the steps going down out of Kanda Station for some alternative to a sprint to present itself. I leaned up against a pillar and closed my eyes.

Thunk, thunk. Thunk. Thunk, thunk. The sound of umbrellas popping open as their owners left the station. A Tokyo obbligato.

If you kidnapped a native of this city who happened to be living in some other part of the world, and blindfolded him and whisked him home, he would know in a minute where he was just by the sounds.

If not by the snatches of conversation in a familiar accent, then by the gonging bell of a delivery bicycle and the intermittent squeak of its brakes as it weaves its way down the street. Or by the scuffle of sandals on the way to the bath, or the negligent *slap slap slap* of sneakers with their backs broken down, or the clatter of the worn wooden geta of a weary kitchen worker. These are Tokyo sounds.

By the *thwack* (pause) *thwack* of a netless game of street badminton. By a street peddler's bored "*Irasshai*" to no one in particular. By the *clackety-clack* of a Hopalong Cassidy ticket-puncher, by the *shush-shush* of ice being shaved, or by the flutter of flags at a used-car lot. By these sounds shall ye know this city.

By the lazy clapping of a cabaret tout, by the shudder of a breeze through a grove of bamboo, by the hellish hammering of metal at a neighborhood foun-

dry whose windows and doors are always wide open
to the street, by the slurring whirl of a pachinko
parlor at full tilt and the interminable Sousa march
which is its invariable accompaniment.

By the clanging of the bells at a railway crossing
as the bamboo poles are lowering and the *greeek* as
the stopped cars pull on their handbrakes. By the
reeeem of locusts, so insistent that they seem intent
on sawing through the tree. By the fairy jangle of
wind bells, the idle drumming of rain on a timpani
tin roof, and the *sluuush* of a car slithering down a
wet alleyway. By the furious shuffling of mah-jongg
tiles from a second-story club at two in the morning.
By the *cling cling cling* as the bell in a family shrine
is struck. By the earthbound strains of Mozart, more
or less, or Chopin, maybe, as practiced by an eleven-
year-old just before dinner.

By the big-brother blare of an olive-green sound
truck as it shoulders its way down the avenue, battle
flags flying, as if noise, only noise would kick the
world back into shape.

By "*Chirigami kokan de gozaimasu*" and "*Saoooo
dake*" and, at election time, the endless introduc-
tions of Suzuki and Ueda and Komatsu and all the
other candidates who are so desperate to make their
names known that they can't say anything else.

By the neighbor's favorite television programs, as
we live so close to each other that their amusements
are perforce ours, too.

By the *peep peep peep peep* and "*Orai, orai*" as a
bus backs up.

By the music-box tune played while the crossing
signal is green. By the subliminal *thud thud* of the
drums of a Bon festival two neighborhoods away. By
the crackling of summer fireworks. By the madcap

rattle rattle clink clink of a *chindonya* band advertising the opening of a new *nomiya*.

By the multilingual spiel of Yodobashi Camera in Shinjuku and the recorded announcement, endlessly repeated, explaining where to buy eyeglasses in Shinbashi.

The police add their own embellishments: "Plate number 14–64, please move your car." And the *woo wang woo wang* of the ambulance is part of the music of Tokyo, too.

The *bosozoku*, the motorcycle hot rodders who come into their own at three in the morning and so become part of our dreams, they are Tokyo. So is the hummingbird buzz of a 50cc bike delivering the morning papers.

At dusk the neighborhood kids stand before each house in turn and sing out *"Hi no yojin"*—Watch out for fire.

These are the sounds of Tokyo.

Who's in Charge Here?

Outside the military, whose organizational structure must be seen to be rock-solid even at the risk of conceptual gridlock, there is no more rigid an organizational hierarchy than that of a kitchen in a first-class Japanese restaurant. An apprentice in a *kaiseki* kitchen spends a year at each of the five stations before rotating back through the same five stations as master apprentice—making a total of ten years before he can call himself *itamae*, literally "one who stands before the chopping board." From there it's still a long haul to *ryori-cho*, or head chef.

Curious to see how a Japanese kitchen operates within these strictures, I arranged to spend a day behind the scenes at Sazanka-so, the extraordinary kaiseki restaurant in the Hotel New Otani's garden. Sazanka-so is where Prime Minister Nakasone invited his summit colleagues for dinner.

When I arrived early in the morning, the apprentices were all at their stations, chopping away with tremendous concentration. Thirty minutes later, the master apprentices strolled in and hung up their coats with great dignity. Thirty minutes later still the assistant chef arrived, cast a cold eye on the proceedings, then busied himself with the construction of the soupe du jour. When he called to the nearest apprentice for a kitchen implement, the apprentice would leap to slap it in his palm.

A good hour later Chef Tanaka appeared. I expected that his appearance would trigger a flurry of hyperactivity, as he was clearly held in great regard by everyone present, and all seemed poised to do his bidding. In fact, though, he washed his hands and without a word went to work slicing radishes with the newest apprentice, the lowest of the low.

In Japan, Chef Tanaka's style of leadership is the norm. By decently obscuring the lines of authority, the terrible problems of rank and power are defused and people of good will are free to get on with their jobs.

Similarly, in the meetings which consume so much time here everyone will free-associate at great length about the problem at hand (or about anything on their mind), the boss presiding with a very light touch, very often keeping mum throughout. There is a general feeling that if a manager should resort to anything so crude as actually *directing* that something be done, he has lost control and the delicate illusion that there is no boss, that everyone is their own boss, would be shattered.

It would seem that the function of a Japanese boss is similar to that ascribed by Bagehot to the British monarchy—to keep the nominal power out of the hands of disputatious politicians, and nothing much more than that.

If the Japanese boss has a job at all, it is to create and nurture an atmosphere in which subordinates are happy and productive and feel their work is appreciated. This might be done in extraordinary ways, of which I will give one example. When my father fell ill I had to tell my boss that it was necessary for me to return to New York for a week. He said, "Yes, I understand." An hour later someone from the personnel department came to my desk and handed me a round-trip airplane ticket. That's a boss.

The only possible problem with the elusive nature of the Japanese executive is that foreign negotiators are apt to be put out when they find out that throughout the negotiating session they have ignored the man who really runs the company. But experienced hands know: in Japan, the boss is the guy who rides away in the black limousine.

The Young Machiavellian's Vade Mecum

Big Tomorrow is a monthly magazine directed to the twenty-year-old Japanese urban male on the make.

It is extraordinary in the sheer detail of the guidance it dispenses on such matters as how to dress for success and for seduction, how to coddle your boss (including even a recommended speech when you are late for work), how to maneuver a young lady into a love hotel (and exactly what to do after you have gotten her there), how to up the odds that chance acquaintances will remember you, and how to build an impressive set of stomach muscles. Four hundred thousand dedicated students of one-upmanship buy a copy of *Big Tomorrow* each month.

A recent article on how to make everybody in your company think you are indispensable is typical. You are advised, first of all, to be sure to greet everyone individually on entering the office in the morning and then, this chore finished, to sit down at your desk and immediately begin making phone calls. (A common error, notes *B.T.*, is to edge into the day's work by perusing the newspapers.)

Young men on the go, advises *B.T.*, should be sure to compliment all female office associates who have changed their hairstyle. On no account should they say "You look different. What happened?" and leave it at that.

When making a phone call, get a reputation for always talking very loudly so your colleagues will be reluctant to be on the phone at the same time. You want your phone calls to be held in awe. Laugh loudly at other people's jokes, no matter how bad. Practice walking faster than anyone else. And make a point of going to lunch with a variety of people, not the same old bunch each day. (If necessary, keep a lunch roster.)

Sending postcards to people after meeting them creates a good impression, but since many people do this it is important that your postcard arrive early, when people remember you best. For this purpose, carry a supply of postcards with you so that you can scribble a note and mail it without delay.

The way you know if your strategy is working is if an office lady brings you tea when you return to the office from an errand *without your asking*.

Another article, called "How to Persuade the Other Fellow in Three Minutes," is equally ruthless and equally flat-footed.

First, dress as the target person and greet him at a close distance of roughly a foot and a half—this will put him off balance. If possible, sit at a round table, which will tend to warm the target person up, and sit with your back to the window so your face will be in the shade and can't be easily read. Slouch down so you will look small and unthreatening; let the target person feel superior. Try to imitate the target person in small ways: if he scratches his head, after a suitable interval you scratch yours, and match the tempo of your speech to his.

Encourage the target person to talk by bobbing your head deeply, until you are sure that he has run out of things to say—wait for the awkward pause. Now he is ripe for convincing.

But perhaps the most poignant recent *Big Tomorrow* article is by Professor Nakazato of Toyo University. The good professor offers a six-day program for getting ahead which can be done at home on your own. The program is especially designed for "shy introverts and those with an inferiority complex." The program is in three parts.

The first part is a series of exercises in interacting socially.

1. Go to the zoo and stare eye-to-eye with an animal *until the animal turns away*. Bears are very good for this exercise.

2. Put up a poster of someone you admire on the wall of your room and in the morning, after bounding vigorously out of bed, stare aggressively into the eyes of the person in the poster for ten seconds while thinking "I can beat you."

3. Get used to talking with strangers. When anyone is passing out leaflets in the street, be sure to take one, look him boldly in the eye and say "Thank you!" Don't buy your soda pop or cigarettes from a vending machine, but go into the store and start a conversation with the proprietor about the weather.

The second part of the program is designed to impart a feeling of superiority.

1. Go up on a high place like a bridge and gaze down at the people passing beneath. Note how small they look.

2. When writing a report to be submitted to one's superior, write in large, bold characters slanted to the right.

3. When passing down a street with not much traffic, walk with a slow gait down the middle of the road with strides of at least three feet.

4. After reading something you don't like in the newspaper violently tear the paper in pieces. Try to find at least one thing you don't like each week.

5. Read autobiographies of famous people, especially the early parts where they acknowledge their mistakes. Think of how you would not have made a mistake if you had been in the same position.

6. Wear a high-class wristwatch.

7. Get yourself a trademark—create yourself a style. For instance, always wear dark glasses. Study Paul Newman in *The Hustler*, Steve McQueen in *Cincinnati Kid*, Marlon Brando in *Streetcar*, or Jean-Paul Belmondo in *Breathless* for hints on how to create a style.

The final part of the program is designed to "get you fired up with an enthusiasm for living."

1. Throw away your monthly calendar. Get a *daily*.

2. Cultivate an unusual hobby so you can gain a reputation as an expert in at least one area. Growing unusual plants is one possibility.

3. Always carry more cash than you'll ever need. And so forth.

Big Tomorrow is a success because it serves as a surrogate older brother, a source of earnest instruction on how to get ahead in a grim, joyless world. The sad thing is that if readers follow *Big Tomorrow*'s big-brotherly advice, they will find themselves ostracized by polite society. *Big Tomorrow* may signal the end of Japanese civilization as we know it.

The Party as Ceremony

Most foreigners like to think of themselves as lovers of fun, quaffers of ale, rollickers until dawn. It is perhaps understandable that people who are used to viewing themselves in this light will tend to look askance at the good burghers of Tokyo, a city where the trains shut down shortly after midnight. Foreigners note that the average Japanese puts in a good 20 percent more hours of work each year than the average fun-loving foreigner, and conclude from this that the Japanese don't know how to relax and let loose, that they don't know how to have a party.

This is very far off the mark. In fact, the Japanese are *party crazy*. The thing is, Japanese parties are different. The purpose of a Japanese party is to celebrate an event. To this end, a party functionary called a *kanji* is appointed. His job is to make sure everyone invited knows where the party is to be held, in Tokyo no simple matter. When everyone has gathered at the appointed place, a hush will fall over the assembly as the kanji clears his throat, announces the purpose of the party just to make sure that everyone is on the same wavelength, and asks the most elevated personage in the group to propose a toast, which is invariably done with good, honest Japanese beer.

When the kanji feels that the event in honor of which the party has been called has been well and truly celebrated, he will announce that the party has come to an end and everyone will immediately depart the premises, perhaps to continue the party on a progressively more informal basis at a series of other places, a process of winding the party down called *nijikai* ("second party"), *sanjikai* ("third party"), and on and on until the last few die-hards run out of steam.

The Japanese have lots of parties because there is a multiplicity of events in the Japanese year which must be celebrated. First off, the fact that it's a new year must be duly marked with a series of *shinnenkai*, New Year's parties, which can take place anytime up until about January 15. A shinnenkai is thrown by one's co-workers and colleagues and acquaintances in other companies with whom your company does business and is a way of easing back to work after the strenuous series of parties held during Shogatsu, the New Year's holidays.

Then there's the *kangeikai,* held to welcome people who have recently joined a section of the company, and the *sobetsukai,* held to bid farewell to anyone leaving the section. In this way anytime anyone moves from one section to another within a company (something which happens with fair frequency), there are at least two parties.

There are *uchiagekai* to celebrate the successful completion of a project; *shokyukai* to congratulate someone on a promotion; and at the end of the year there is a two-week round of *bonenkai* ("year-forgetting parties"). Not to mention the informal parties that take place every evening in Tokyo's thousands of cozy little drinking places called *nomiya.*

And those are just the parties with fellow workers. There is a whole other series of parties generated by family events, from *shussaniwai* to celebrate the birth of a child to *hoji,* a long series of parties to commemorate a death. Every neighborhood has its grand communal blast in the summer and the whole country knocks off for a week of parties during the Obon season. We have parties to celebrate the blooming of the plum, the blooming of the cherry, and the beauty of the autumn moon. We have a party when children become three and five and seven, and when they turn twenty. We have a big party when anyone turns sixty.

It sometimes seems that the fundamental reason for the whole elaborate structure called Japanese culture is simply to provide a framework for a regular round of parties.

Breakfast in Tokyo

I hear that New Yorkers who want to enlist some-one's support have taken to inviting them to a "power breakfast." The main attraction of a power breakfast seems to be that the host can put the whammy on his guest before the poor fellow's defense mechanisms are fully in gear.

The constant jockeying for advantage that goes on in New York must make for exciting living. The idea of power breakfasting is still foreign to our city, which for a world capital seems remarkably inno-cent of intrigue.

Tokyo breakfasts are devoid of strategic probing or even of much conversation. They are for the most part slapdash affairs eaten in a terrible rush, as a soldier might bolt his rations before combat. Com-pared to a Tokyo breakfast, the standard breakfast where I grew up of eggs, sausages, and blueberry muffins is positively rococo.

In fact, breakfast here is so undervalued an event that there is really no such thing as a standard Tokyo breakfast.

Outside of a high-class hotel, the closest you can come to anything which might decently break a fast is the breakfast served at a good Japanese inn. Unfor-tunately, Tokyo is not blessed with a wealth of good Japanese inns. Even if it were, their habit of present-ing a soy-sauced cold fried egg as a side dish has a way of spiking an appetite not yet ready to fight back.

There's not much chance these days of getting a good breakfast at home, either. The miso soup, rice, and pickles (and maybe cold fried egg) which constitute the classic home breakfast in Japan are labor-intensive and are proving too much trouble to prepare for a modern urban family in perpetual motion. And home versions of Western breakfasts can be very bizarre.

The set breakfast offered by the coffee shops is out on a limb all its own. It might consist of a quarter head of lettuce crowned with a swirl of bottled mayonnaise, a two-inch-thick piece of toasted white bread, a tiny container of a yogurt-like beverage, and a cold fried egg. It is difficult to think what the inspiration for such a combination of ingredients might have been. One imagines that years ago the proprietor of a Tokyo coffeehouse took a whirlwind tour of a dozen countries and on his return to Tokyo attempted to reconstruct what he had eaten each morning, but he could remember only vaguely.

The station kiosks do a roaring breakfast business with their tuna, egg-salad, and pork-cutlet sandwiches, which have been assembled the night before in some underground sandwich factory. The sandwiches are washed down with strawberry- or coffee-flavored milk. The whole process, including unwrapping the sandwiches, takes two minutes.

An early-morning bowl of noodles devoured while standing at a counter is even faster. A noodle shop in Shinjuku Station sells tickets through a vending machine, relieving customers of the necessity of informing the counterman of what they fancy. Customers just slap down their ¥300 ticket and their bowl of noodles is slid down the counter. An experienced noodle-fancier can inhale a bowl in thirty seconds flat. Some of the larger companies run cafeterias for their employees where a bowl of noodles can be had for ¥90, although here there exists a serious disadvantage in that people are expected to consume their meal while sitting down.

Bakeries near the stations open early for those in the mood for beanpaste croissants and mixed-vegetable purée in flaky pastry. The hopelessly depraved content themselves with a drink of 10 percent peach nectar from the vending machine on the street.

One has to say that the idea of breakfasting in Tokyo is an idea still evolving. At least one hopes it is evolving.

The Real Reason
Japan Is No. 1

Several years ago, at the peak of all the palaver about Japanese management techniques, *New York Times'* columnist James Reston came to Tokyo to see for himself what all the fuss was about. A perceptive man, it didn't take him long to put the thing in perspective. He noted that all you had to do to see what distinguishes Japanese goods in the world market was to drive your car into any Tokyo gas station.

What happens, of course, is that a team of attendants as well drilled as the operating-room team of a surgeon descends on your car. While one attendant fills the tank, the others clean your windshield, headlights, and outside mirrors, empty and wash out the ashtrays, scrub the floor mats, adjust the antenna, and give you a briefing on traffic conditions in the direction of your destination. Then they will halt traffic so that you can ease your car back out onto the road without anxiety.

The gas station wants you to come back to them when you need gas, so they will do everything they can to keep you from straying to the competition.

When you buy a car in Tokyo, you declare yourself a Toyota, Mazda, or Daihatsu creature. Thenceforth, you can expect your dealer to cultivate you like a rare plant.

He'll send you birthday cards, drive around to your house any new model he thinks you might like to take a drive in, pamper your present vehicle by calling you up when it is due for servicing, then sending a man around to pick it up (leaving you another car in its place), servicing it, washing it, waxing it, and then returning it all in a matter of hours. He wants to maximize his chances of selling you your next car.

In Tokyo, competition is crushing, brutal, mad.

In 1982 Yamaha had the nerve to challenge Honda for supremacy in the motorcycle market. James Abegglen in his book *Kaisha* says that at this point the president of Honda "issued a battle cry—'*Yamaha wo tsubusu!*'—which can be variously translated as 'We will crush/break/smash/squash/butcher/slaughter/destroy Yamaha.'" Over the next eighteen months, Honda introduced eighty-one new motorcycle models, swamping poor Yamaha, who only managed to produce thirty-four new models.

Every April, the soft-drink companies launch their new products for the summer season with a barrage of carefully coordinated television commercials and giant posters in the train and subway stations. Hundreds of fancifully named new soft drinks are loaded into the city's hundreds of thousands of vending machines, which attempt to engage the scurrying pedestrian with whistles and bells and flashing lights and the recorded blandishments of sirens. Most of these new soft drinks are knocked out of the market by the end of the month.

Vespa, the Italian motor scooter, had a nice little niche in the Tokyo transportation market all to itself until a few years ago when a Japanese company produced an alternative. By the end of the year there were a couple of dozen Japanese motor scooters vying for attention. Now there are hundreds, and new variations come on the market almost daily.

Japanese manufacturers in this fiercely competitive market know they must gauge consumer preferences with great accuracy or they will be winnowed out without ceremony. (The bankruptcy rate in Japan is much higher than in the U.S.) Electronics companies regularly send new employees to work on the front lines for a couple of weeks in Akihabara, the frenzied electronics marketplace in downtown Tokyo that sells 10 percent of all the electronics gear sold in Japan. The diaries the new employees keep during this time are pored over by their company's designers, engineers, and marketing people for clues to the mood of the Tokyo consumer. If a product looks as though it's going to float, a series of variations will immediately be put on the market in order to consolidate market share and sustain the momentum.

In Japan, even products that in other countries would not normally be subject to direct assault by the competition are fair game. Your friendly local paperboy will join the battle for newspaper circulation by offering gifts to households who will switch their allegiance, an arrangement which causes some families to switch their daily newspaper regularly every few months.

Tokyo is the greatest testing lab for product viability in the world. For a product to succeed in this environment, it's got to be first class. The products Japanese manufacturers select for promotion in export markets are simply those that have survived the competitive crunch here.

More than anything else, this is the reason for the success of Japanese products in the world marketplace.

"Are You Busy?"

The usual quick greeting in the halls of the place where I work is *Isogashii desu ka?*—"Are you busy?" I used to answer this inquiry with an offhand "No, not particularly," until it dawned on me that that response invariably caused the inquirer to put on a face of great sympathetic concern, just as if I had answered, "Alas, my doctor has told me that I have a weak heart and I must not strain myself."

Where I work, which I suppose is a reasonably typical Japanese office, not to be busy is to be deprived of one of life's great joys. Everyone here thinks that anybody who is not busy is *adrift*.

I know what busy is. Busy is when you are a combination lifeguard, beach boy, parking-lot attendant, soda jerk, and dishwasher at a popular Cape Cod beach resort on a Labor Day weekend. Busy is what a Kiosk Lady is during rush hour, responding to requests from a dozen customers at once and spewing out change like an automatic ticket dispenser. Busy is what a tuna auctioneer at Tsukiji is during his daily stint in the limelight when he sells a thousand tons of fresh fish in twenty minutes. Busy is being engaged in a frenzy of activity. Busy is having no time for reflection.

The pace of work in any Tokyo office I've ever visited could not by any stretch of the imagination be described by the English word "busy." Most people spend their time either sunk in deep reflection or in desultory discussions over cups of green tea. Is this yet another instance of a word meaning one thing to foreigners and something rather different to Japanese? Like "teacher" (which in Japanese means *God*) or "obligation" (which in Japanese means *God's will*) or "foreigner" (which in Japanese means *person from Mars*).

I have yet to come across a Japanese who is willing to admit that he is not busy. A Japanese fly fisherman lazing on the bank of a mountain stream, his cap pulled down over his eyes, if nudged and asked if he is busy, would cock his head and mutter in the affirmative.

From this, I think we must conclude that Japanese live a furious interior life, that in fact, though their body may appear to be in repose, their brain is in overdrive, churning through some complex problem, and that "busy," therefore, means in Japanese not much more than being alive and ticking.

How curious the vagaries of cultural values! My own cultural tradition has caused me to think of "busyness" in vaguely perjorative terms. "Busy" is what my grandmother used to call a stretch of wallpaper that was too obviously straining for effect. In my office in New York, to say that someone was terribly busy was to suggest that he didn't have a very firm grip on his job.

At my university, we would go to great lengths to avoid the appearance of being busy. We cultivated a reputation for languid brilliance. Stephen Potter tells of the Harvard undergrad who studied furiously for examinations in a rented room off campus with his shirt off and a sunlamp turned on, so when it came time to sit the exam he could breeze into the examination hall ten minutes late, claiming he had just got off the plane from Jamaica, and ace the exam, turning in his blue books thirty minutes early, then asking the monitor to please excuse him because he had a tennis date. That was our ideal, that was the game we played.

The ideal at a Japanese university seems exactly the reverse: while keeping up a front of busyness—not academic so much as social, it is true—most Japanese undergraduates float through their four years.

In the end, though, I suppose it doesn't make a great deal of difference whether you espouse the busy or the languid mode, as long as you do it with style.

Only in Tokyo

I can't imagine any of the following scenes (all of which really took place) happening anywhere but in Tokyo. They have in common a certain solemn wackiness which may be this city's single most endearing characteristic.

—Two students in somber school uniforms and spiky haircuts board the Yamanote Line at Shibuya with an enormous drum. They just manage to fit it through the door of the last car and they have to keep it next to the door or it would completely block the aisle. (There are signs in the stations which indicate that surfboards must not be taken on the trains, but nobody said anything about drums.) The drum is as great a presence on the train as would be Lady Godiva, but nobody evidences the slightest interest. Finally, a little boy breaks away from his mother to go up to the drum and flick a finger against the drumhead, causing the drum to give off a timid ping. One of the students takes a large drumstick from his back pocket and hands it to the boy, who grins and belts the drumhead as hard as he can. The sound rumbles through the train. Comes an announcement from the conductor at the back of the train: "No-drum-playing time is between seven to nine in the morning and four to six in the evening. We request your kind cooperation in this regard. Thank you."

—Kenwood has a large audio equipment showroom on the street running between Yurakucho and Marunouchi which is lined with trees and banks. Every noon a woman in a Kenwood jumper seats herself like a schoolmistress behind a desk and with great dignity presents a recorded concert. If you drop in you will see about forty bank and insurance company functionaries in subfusc coat and tie sitting in ranks of fold-up chairs, scanning copies of *Nihon Keizai* or *Kabushiki Shinbun*, occasionally swinging an ankle in sympathy to the surging rhythms of "Afternoon of a Fawn" or "Bolero" played very loudly through a huge set of speakers. It is like sitting in church listening to an erotic hymn. The concert is timed to end just before one o'clock, so everyone can get back to their desks on time.

—In Ginza 4-chome, right next to the police station, a block from the multistoried off-track betting establishment, is a small park where on Sundays a middle-aged gentleman comes to practice his bagpipe. I imagine he comes here because his family has hinted that their home is too small to allow such a wonderful instrument to be fully appreciated. So he comes to this park, dressed in full bagpipe-playing regalia—kilt, sporran, tam-o'-shanter, tartan stockings and spats, and footgear with silver buckles—to move back and forth with a stately tread wheezing out over and over again "Scotland the Brave." Most of the time his only audience will be an unshaven connoisseur of saké who applauds loudly at the end of each effort and whom the bagpiper studiously ignores.

—In another park, this one near my house, a park with no greenery whatsoever, only a set of swings and a bench, I saw the other day four men playing tennis on a patch of bare soil. It did not matter to them that there was no net where they played or lines to indicate whether the ball was in or out. It was an entirely theoretical game, the point of which was not to ace your opponent but to keep the ball nicely in play, just as if there had been a proper net and lines and an attentive referee on a perch. Each of the players wore immaculate tennis whites and on the bench they had left their extra rackets and towels to bury their faces in between sets.

How the City Forges Character

I have an idea that the reason Tokyoites are so enamored of precision—a Tokyo shopgirl wraps a package as though it were going to be presented to God and you get the idea that anyone whose job it is to stack boxes or count change puts in an hour or two of practice before reporting for work in the morning—is that the city simply *imposes* this frame of mind on everyone who lives here.

The fundamental molding force that makes Tokyoites what they are is the city's brutish crowdedness. Because there isn't a lot of room, everyone is used to living with a very small margin of error. The madcap desperado method of driving that prevails in most of South America, for instance, just wouldn't work here, where two buses pass on an ordinary street with a four-inch leeway between their sideview mirrors. In Tokyo, a four-inch margin is a piece of cake.

In fact, mothers roll their infants in precision-made strollers six inches or less from the passing traffic without giving it a second thought.

The trains roar into the stations at 60 kph (a bit under 38 mph), the waiting throng a mere half a step away from the edge of the platform and oblivion. No one has ever fallen from the platform, though occasionally some poor soul, sick of precision, jumps.

Crowdedness forms the Tokyo character in other ways, too.

People learn to be very calculating, because in Tokyo if your urban strategy is not well honed, you will be trampled. People maneuver to board a train through a certain door of a certain car. They do this so that when they reach their station they will be lined up with the stairs, and thus well positioned for the dash up.

Tokyo families are tightly knit and very supportive, because it takes teamwork to survive in this city. Either a family or the services of a well-drilled staff are required to take care of the extended and involved negotiations involving the laundry, the landlord, the telephone company, the bank, the town hall, the television and automobile repair shops, the fish market, the newspaper delivery boy, and a hundred other detail-mongering negotiating partners. The city has a way of instilling a fierce group consciousness, because people soon find out that going it alone very often means not going at all.

Tokyoites become nature lovers of an extraordinary intensity, because in the city a glimpse of nature is as rare as an eclipse. At Shizen Kyoikuen, the nature park in Meguro, you can see people down on their knees examining newly sprouted mushrooms and training cameras with enormous lenses on drowsy spiders in their webs. When Tokyoites can't find nature, they simulate it: witness the tape of bird chirps played during rush hour in Shinjuku Station. In this way, the line between what's real and what's merely conjured up becomes blurred in the Tokyo consciousness. Fantasy becomes real, and sneaking off to a love hotel built like the Taj Mahal is done in the same spirit as residents of other cities go out to buy the evening papers.

The city forces us to be patient, because there is nothing else to do, and hardworking, because, well because everyone else works hard and if you don't you will be ostracized, very subtly, of course.

To see the extent the city molds the character of its residents, all you have to do is observe Tokyoites on a trip outside the city. If they are not accustomed to the differences between Tokyo and the rest of the world, they lose their identities and go gaga.

Tokyo Revives the Adventure of Travel

The *New York Times* recently published a bar graph showing that it costs twice as much to have a suit cleaned in Tokyo as in Paris, the world's next most expensive suit-cleaning city. Well, yes. Tokyo is also an expensive city for a cup of coffee and for a melon to be given as a gift. If you conclude on the basis of this evidence, however, that nobody without easy access to a mint can live in Tokyo, you will have fallen prey to what we call around here the Melon Fallacy. Just look around you: millions of people of modest means sustain life in Tokyo without apparent strain. They just don't have their suits cleaned very often and go easy on the coffee and the melons.

Unfortunately, in the lobbies of the grand hotels you can now hear visitors vying to top each other's stories of unbelievable prices, and so the rumor that Tokyo is no place for the ordinary tourist feeds on itself. Travel magazines published abroad respond to the slimming of the touristic influx by running fewer and fewer illustrated articles about the quaint Japanese countryside and this causes a further dropping off. It has reached the point where if something is not done to set matters straight the only foreigners visiting town will be foreign airline flight crews and trade missions.

It is perfectly obvious that Tokyo will be on the expensive side if you insist on treating it as just another world capital. The check for a Western breakfast in a top-flight Tokyo hotel will give you indigestion for the rest of the day. But how many Tokyoites start the day with ham and eggs at the Imperial? Instead, for breakfast have a bowl of buckwheat noodles at a stand-up counter in one of the stations. You'll be in good, if jostling, company and it won't run you more than ¥300.

While you're at it, don't stay at a sleek hotel at all. How many Japanese who have come to Tokyo from the northern provinces for a day on the town stay at a hotel like the Okura? Zero. They can't afford it any more than you can. They stay at a "business" hotel or a rough-and-ready ryokan near Ueno Station, and it costs them ¥5,000 a night, breakfast included.

To get around town, avoid taxis and take the subways and buses. Tokyo is a great city for walking and gawking, constant theater. In fact, to come to Tokyo to see the famous sights is a misguided strategy. With the possible exception of Sensoji, we don't *have* any famous sights. Come to Tokyo to walk around; it costs nothing. Or go to the bicycle races; it costs ¥50.

Other easy-on-the-pocket amusements are pachinko (the *definition* of a cheap way to pass the time), a stroll through the Ginza (where at the Ginza Pocket Park, for example, you can listen for nothing to a concert on the world's only gas organ), and a visit to a public bath, which costs just ¥230 for an all-day soak.

When you get hungry, just go where everyone else is going and order what they do. *Teishoku* lunch and *bento* boxed lunch are bargains, sometimes as low as ¥500. Sushi plucked from a moving conveyor belt at any of the branches of Genroku-zushi around town cost just ¥100 apiece, with all the tea you can drink. That's the way Tokyo eats. A good cheap place is bound to be crowded and noisy and bursting with life. In the evening, drop into a little Japanese bar and order a flask of saké for a few hundred yen. The experience is *guaranteed* to be memorable. Then, as the evening winds down, settle in at a *yatai* street cart for a bowl of *oden* stew for ¥800 at the outside.

Of course, you'll want to buy souvenirs and presents. Don't buy the sort of thing you can buy anywhere. Visit one of the city's many flea markets for old signs, crusted military decorations of the Crimean campaign, elaborate antique hair ornaments, used silk kimono (available for a few thousand yen), and other curiosities. Subway posters, well-printed on good paper, make provocative wall-hangings back home, if you can pry the thumbtacks out without getting caught.

In short, approach Tokyo as though you were a nineteenth-century traveler entering Timbuktu. If you disdain the posh hotels and credit-card restaurants and ready-made tours, and just wander and look, you will find it a great adventure, and not expensive at all.

Japanese Inventiveness

One of the quick-drawn taunts that all Japanese have to countenance—just as every American must come to grips with the rest of the world's insisting that all Americans are born chewing gum—is that the Japanese race is incapable of invention. It is easy to see how this idea got started. When the emperor Meiji dispatched a cadre of bright young men to Europe and the United States with the mission of discovering what all the hoopla about technology was about and they came back with blueprints of suspension bridges, models of steam locomotives, and an outline of what a national banking system looked like, it was inevitable that they be accused of copying. They *were* copying. The thing is, once someone's given you the idea of a bridge, all you can do is refine it. You can't reinvent it.

What gets overlooked in the Most Inventive Nation sweepstakes, though, is that the Japanese in fact are *enormously* inventive on a scale that doesn't seem to count. You don't get points, apparently, for devising simple solutions to everyday problems.

Velcro may not be a Japanese invention, but using Velcro strips in place of shoelaces certainly is. So is the license plate whose numbers light up, the bus stop that announces where the bus is, and the extendable drinking straw to get to the bottom of the glass. So is the postcard whose message is covered by a thin aluminum flap, allowing writers of Japanese postcards to be as indiscrete as writers of letters.

Other Japanese inventions so far unappreciated by the world at large are vertical briefcases with a shoulder strap, snaps in the cuffs of trousers, and cards on a ring for learning vocabulary. Any foreigner who has ever been able to bring himself to try it must acknowledge that slurping is easily the best method of consuming a bowl of noodles. The Japanese discovered long ago that it is aerodynamically feasible to ride a bicycle while holding an open umbrella, while cyclists of the rest of the world just get wet.

It is an old Japanese invention to seal a bottle of soda pop from the inside with a marble, to have an office *hanko* automatically ink itself after each use, to keep feet warm by a *kotatsu*, to keep sweat off the brow with a *hachimaki*, and to transport baggage by the sensible, cheap, colorful, and totally collapsible suitcase called the *furoshiki*.

A magazine called *Mono* devotes fifty pages each month to new inventions, like a pith helmet with a built-in solar-powered fan and a tape recorder designed to float in a swimming pool with its speakers pointing down so underwater swimmers can listen to Handel, but the magazine just can't keep up with the volume of inventions.

My company receives from its thirty thousand employees a quarter million wildly inventive suggestions each year. Every year a Tokyo department store stages an exhibition of inventions dreamed up by housewives during the previous year (like a chopping block on an incline so things fall off only in one direction), which is covered by the press as an annual event.

Look at all the ways of getting things done the Japanese have invented—the *ringi* system, the *koban* system, and just-in-time logistics; in ways of sustaining oneself—sushi, Calpis, and tempura ice cream; in artforms—haiku, Kabuki, incense inhalation, and the artful counting of banknotes. That's *invention*.

But now technology has reached a level of sophistication that makes it extremely difficult for even an inventive genius to make a new breakthrough. Invention of a new technology has become a matter of doggedly probing the potential of a complex idea—that's why the process is called research and development—and it is here that the Japanese come into their own, by breaking an idea down into small bits and subjecting each bit to the most painstaking examination.

The Japanese are now being granted patents at a higher rate per capita than any country in the world. What is more, Japanese patents are being cited more often than American patents in applications for new patents, suggesting that Japanese patents are the fruit of more seminal work.

Leisure: Key to the Western Mind and All That

I see that Dr. Tadao Ishikawa, president of Keio University, has acknowledged what some of us have long suspected, that students at universities hereabouts don't spend an overwhelming amount of time with the books. "Leisure land" is how he characterizes Japanese universities, a sort of suburb, one gathers, of Disneyland. The good doctor goes on to say:

"But I say a leisure land is fine. The reason is that before entering a university, students today have sacrificed much of their growth as human beings because of the excessive study for entrance examinations. That is why there is a phase that upon entering a university, they seek to make a recovery as human beings through enjoyable extracurricular activities or association with friends. If they carried on university life grimly as merely an extension of their senior high school days, what kind of a world would this be?"

Under the circumstances, a grim world indeed. I have to say, though, that I am equally unattracted by Dr. Ishikawa's picture of the leisurely life—an academic arcadia inhabited by students so exhausted that it is all they can do to stagger down to the local coffeehouse for a quiet game of video mayhem with an equally shattered classmate. The reason Dr. Ishikawa's leisure land does not appeal to me (and I am one who puts a good deal of faith in the life-enhancing power of leisure) is that what he means by "leisure" and what I mean are not coincident.

What I mean by leisure is simply time spent pursuing one's own interests (you know, composing symphonies, climbing hitherto unscaled peaks, engineering breathtaking scientific breakthroughs, etc.) at one's own (presumably unflustered) pace. By this definition, the ideal life is one that includes a maximum of leisure.

Contrast this with Dr. Ishikawa's vision of leisure as a momentary break in the routine of banging one's head against the wall, as equivalent to the groggy interval between the rounds of a slugging match. Leisure is a blessed relief, leisure is sleep, leisure is, ultimately, death.

Dr. Ishikawa is not alone in this formulation. Most of Tokyo sees leisure as an enforced lull in activity occurring, as if by governmental fiat, on those days marked in red on the national calendar, when the trains run on a funny schedule. It does not help that there is no word in Japanese for *leisure*. *Asobi* suggests childlike, mindless play—pachinko for example. *Yoka* literally means something like extra time on your hands. One would think that *leisure* tricked out in *katakana—rejaa*—would be a reasonable approximation, but in fact *rejaa* carries the clear implication of ritual family recreation, such as a dutiful Sunday drive in a slow-moving traffic jam to a picnic place and back.

Of course leisure in the Western sense of a life fulfilled is not a concept totally alien to Japan—one thinks of the tea ceremony and other arts pursued in the natural flow of life—but when there is no word for a concept, it is difficult to rally around it, to cultivate it. There has always been this dichotomy in Japan between work (which can be and very often is a rather relaxed state of being, even if it occupies twelve hours a day, six days a week, fifty weeks a year) and non-work, or *yasumi*. The switch is either on or off, so leisure becomes a kind of recuperative medicine, like cod-liver oil, for debilitated souls to partake of before pulling themselves together and re-entering the normal, healthy world of work.

It occurs to me that in the end, the achievement of a civilization is measured not by the quality of its laws, or machines, or architecture, or fireworks, but by the quality of the leisure it inspires, which is another way of saying quality of life. Looked at this way, it seems that the ultimate purpose of a university liberal arts education is to prepare one for living a life of leisure. A noble aim.

3. Fantasies

Touching Up the Local Color

For some time now the Japan National Tourist Organization has been concerned that foreigners who venture to Tokyo for a traditional three-day whirlwind tour of the city's sights may be going home disappointed. No geishas, no picturesque teahouses along the Sumida River, and damn few kimonos.

It doesn't help that the recent funny business with the yen has caused the average foreign tourist to calculate in advance the cost of even a mad bowl of noodles.

One understands the JNTO's concern. It's not likely that tourists will go very far out of their way to inspect sights like Tokyo's massive Ark Hills complex, a recent eruption on the skyline which has become something of a symbol of the direction in which the city is sliding—sleek cement, chromium revolving doors, and a theatrical waterfall: Tokyo's own Rockefeller Center. This is not what attracts tourists, who can see pretty much the same thing in dozens of cities where the noodles are a good deal cheaper. No, as tourist bait nothing beats indigenous quaintness, a quality which in Tokyo is rapidly being worn away.

As a countermeasure, the JNTO has set up in Takadanobaba a new educational institution called the Nippon Kyu-Bunka Kenkyusho, or Japan Institute of Ancient Culture. The purpose of this school (or so I am informed by a usually fairly reliable source) is to recruit and train young people (who would otherwise be tempted to take up a workaday job like computer programmer or financial analyst) in the quaint urban occupations of goldfish seller, tofu hawker, back-scrubber in the public baths, and the like.

The graduates of the school are to be strategically located throughout the city in places tourists are likely to frequent to imbue the city with color so the visitors will take back home with them stories of the charming shaved-ice stands in the lobby of the Imperial Hotel and the colorful cutthroat *jinrikisha* jockeys lying in wait outside the Akasaka night spots. The project has the full backing, I understand, of the highest councils.

A top priority is the reinstallation at the foot of the escalators in the department stores of the ladies who used to bow and murmur sweet welcomes to customers as they were whisked upstairs, all the while running a handkerchief along the moving handrail to keep it unsullied. Tourists used to regard these ladies with the same degree of awe as tourists to London regard the Beefeaters. The school has a platoon of them now in training.

Also in training is squad of lads who will be able to balance several dozen bowls of *katsudon* on a tray on their shoulder with one hand while slaloming a bicycle through back streets full of pedestrians with the other. After graduating, these lads will be assigned to well-populated areas of the city where their job will be to careen back and forth through the crowd with their tray of dummy bowls of *donburi* teetering tantalizingly.

Cashiers now being trained in the flamboyant use of specially resonant abacuses will be assigned to reckon up the bill at selected French restaurants, and the menus of these restaurants are to be written by brush by a team of calligraphers being trained in amusing variant spellings.

Our street carts, whose standard of culinary preparations has (let us admit) slipped a bit over the years, are soon to be staffed by graduates of the school with a solid grounding in the proper preparation of *takoyaki* and *oden*, and they will have as well the benefit of a short course in charmingly broken English late-night raconteurship.

Kamishibaiya storytellers are now in training. Their audience will be assured by the government-sponsored passing out of free candy to the kids.

Tourists are no longer to be denied the thrill of ferreting out a back-alley bargain. Shops selling (last year's) electronic equipment are to be set up under the railroad tracks, just like old times, and the graduates of the school who will staff the shops are being instructed in how to put on a great show of being routed by crafty bargainers from abroad.

All graduates of the school are pledged to take their nightly ablutions at their local public baths, where they will get a discount, and to proceed to the bath with a swagger, dressed in *yukata* and geta and carrying their bathing gear in a wooden (not plastic) bowl of government issue.

It is felt that this program will in time assure that Tokyo is again perceived by tourists as one of the mysterious cities of the East and one of the classic travel experiences. When this has been achieved, Phase II of the plan will be launched: police boxes are to set off a ten-minute fireworks display every Wednesday evening and hundreds of thousands of fireflies now being bred are to be let loose. Firefly nets and cages are to be issued to everyone under eight.

Tour to End All Tours

It may be that you experience the same feeling of being cornered that I do when I receive a call from someone who breathlessly announces that they are about to arrive in Tokyo and that old Sam Remarbler (or some similar name that only dimly resonates in the memory) told them that they must without fail be sure to look up old Rick Kennedy.

Of course one does enjoy showing innocents from abroad around the city—the message one subtly manages to convey is: This is my city; my days are full of wonder; I have had a fairly substantial hand in all this. The visitors' state of shell-shocked frenzy does solicit a certain sympathy and they do sometimes bring with them useful gifts.

Still, because these instant acquaintances never seem to find the time to write to introduce themselves and give reasonable notice of their arrival, I always feel, having consented to meet them and show them The Real Tokyo, that I have committed myself to a blind date.

Accordingly, I have over the years devised a tour designed to give the impression that while old Rick certainly goes out of his way to show the city at its most charming and intimate, Tokyo is in fact the world's most overrated city. After having taken my tour, you see, visitors are most unlikely to suggest to their Tokyo-bound friends that they should give old Rick a ring.

It helps that most flights from abroad arrive at Narita in the early evening. Graciously meeting the visitor at the airport, I first escort him or her to the airport chapel for the one-hour traditional Shinto ceremony thanking the gods for a safe trip. The ceremony, which I rig up beforehand with obliging college students, involves much banging together of pieces of wood and has as its climax the ritual sipping of a single sacred thimble of saké. It being now about 8 P.M., we adjourn to the airport cafeteria for a dish of traditional curry rice.

We then take the local train to Ueno. On the way I point out several dozen colorful *kanji* and delineate their historical development on a series of flash cards which I give to the visitor, suggesting that the lot be committed to memory as soon as possible.

It's ten o'clock when we arrive in Ueno. We board the Yamanote Line, which I describe as "the best quick introduction to the city," although at this hour, of course, we can see nothing but colorful flickering neon. We take one complete turn before alighting at Shinjuku Station for a fifteen-minute walk to the colorful traditional ryokan called Furujuku, which seems to accept only backpacking foreigners.

The bath at Furujuku is rusty and the place specializes in breakfasts of cold fried eggs and instant miso soup enlivened by chunks of boiled sweet potato. I usually try to arrange for a copy of *Shipping and Trade News* to be slipped under the visitor's door in the morning so I can later characterize it as a good rundown of what's going on.

About eight o'clock the next morning I pick the visitor up for a trip to Tsukiji market to view the famous cabbage auction. Then to Kappabashi to inspect the plastic replicas of spaghetti and strawberry shortcake. This is bound to deflate any appetite which may have survived the jet lag, so I now suggest we have lunch, preferably a ¥350 *tonkatsu teishoku*, cold fried pork cutlet served with a mound of shredded cabbage. "You're very lucky," I point out. "It's the cabbage season."

During lunch I outline a number of possibilities for the afternoon. We could visit the Tobacco and Salt Museum in Shibuya, for example, or take in the famous wax museum at the base of Tokyo Tower, or visit Nihonbashi, the bridge from which all distances in Japan were traditionally measured (the bridge now being ideally located, for my purposes, under the Shuto Expressway). If possible, I try to have a Japanese high-school student accost us at this point and stick with us the rest of the day practicing nineteenth-century English proverbs.

If the visitor is culturally inclined, I might suggest we take in a Gagaku concert, performed by a battery of ancient instruments which have a total range of half an octave, or that interminable Noh play in which the total action consists of the central character tapping his foot several times.

Still another possibility, particularly attractive if the ground is covered by a heavy mist, is to go out to the banks of the Tama River to watch Tokyo's future jazz greats practicing in the marshy vastness their trombones and clarinets.

Of course, if the season is right, we could visit a temple for *setsubun*, the colorful ceremony in which devils are exorcised by having beans thrown at them; *harikuyo*, the annual memorial service at Sensoji for old pins and needles; or *asagaoichi*, the market which allows the visitor to take his or her pick of thousands of pots of morning glories. All very colorful and traditional.

If after all this they are *still* game, I take them up Fuji—at night, lighting our way with paper lanterns, with the honored guest being given the privilege of wearing straw sandals while climbing this most sacred of all mountains.

Rooftop Golf

From a Chuo Line train rumbling along at rooftop level through the western suburbs of Nakano, Asagaya, and Koenji, one sees endless acres of somberly tinted tiled roofs stretching unbroken in all directions to the horizon. This part of the city is as flat as a Dutch landscape.

In order not to tempt the earthquake god, dwellings are built no higher than two stories, but because this is Tokyo, they are built so close together that the eaves of many houses are tucked under the eaves of their neighbors. One could walk for miles, stepping from roof to roof, with no more trouble than picking one's way across a stream from boulder to boulder.

It is here, on the roof of an all-night sauna, that the Musashi Plain Country Club has its clubhouse. The MPCC, founded in Showa 57 (1982), sees itself as an alternative to the high-priced golf clubs in Hakone and Izu whose members view a round of golf as a necessary preliminary to any serious negotiating session, and also as an alternative to the neighborhood driving courses, protected from the workaday world by huge nets, where devotees of the game come at all hours of the night and day to belt buckets of balls toward bull's-eyes on the back wall.

The MPCC pro, Angus Mochizuki, has developed a new version of the ancient and honorable game which particularly suits the urban geography of Tokyo: the course is laid out entirely on roofs. But let Angus explain:

"It is indeed a pleasure to come up here on the roof of the Super Suds Building when the morning air is fresh. You can clearly see the skyscrapers of Shinjuku. Every couple of minutes a train full of worthies commuting in to fill up those buildings goes by, right through the middle of our course.

"I usually wait until the rush hour is over before teeing off for my daily practice round. The first hole is four hundred yards. It's a little tricky because if you aren't careful you can hook into the clotheslines on the roof of Las Vegas Pachinko, and the bonsai plants on the roof of Suzuki Real Estate are a kind of sand trap.

"The next several holes are pretty routine—just take note of the lumberyard over there, a natural hazard. On the seventh hole we try to keep away from the house with the large tin roof strung with barbed wire: a piano teacher lives on the top floor and she is not so happy when someone plays her roof in the middle of a lesson. Otherwise, it is pretty much like a conventional course. Most of the greens are on flat roofs, and the seventeenth hole even has a grass green, kept up by the florist who owns the building as a kind of public service.

"No special skill is required for rooftop golf, but there's a lot of wind up here. Airplanes and pigeons and advertising balloons can be distractions if you're not used to them. Of course, if a ball rolls off the course into the street below, you lose a stroke, but the balls are a little different from conventional golf balls: they are made of the same substance as those little red octopuses that crawl so spastically down vertical surfaces and are hawked so languidly by street vendors in the Ginza. Our balls kind of stick, instead of bounce. People tell me that when a ball hits their roof, it sounds a bit like a loose snowball. Sort of a *splat*.

"There is some interest in Osaka in the sport but Osaka people, you know, are so serious. They have the idea that if you want to play a quick round of golf you have to put on your patent-leather golf shoes with little chromium spikes on the bottom, and your single kangaroo-leather glove, and travel outside the city to a rolling, green sward. In Tokyo, well, we just grab the clubs and go upstairs."

The Chuo Line Caper

About forty people were involved initially, but there was a gradual shakeout of the fainthearted as D-day approached. In the end just twenty-five stalwarts took part. They were of all types: there was a freelance poster designer, a racing-motorcycle mechanic, a yacht salesman, the streetwise owner of a sophisticated supper club, a dentist on the lookout for action, and, quite appropriately, an artist who specializes in oversized canvases. They came together over a period of six months, the idea being proposed in a whisper, and either rejected in horrified tones, or considered, toyed with, and passed on.

The Planning Committee was divided into seven working groups: the Design W.G., the Training

W.G., the Paint W.G., the Security W.G., the Surveillance W.G., the New York Coordinating W.G., and the Publicity W.G.

The Design Working Group produced one-fiftieth-scale sketches of several proposed designs, then, once a consensus had been reached, broke the final design down into components which the individual limners could duplicate on the portion of the train assigned to them in twenty minutes or less.

The Paint Working Group ran tests to determine the most appropriate paint and method of application.

The Training Working Group held weekly candle-lit practice sessions, which they timed with a stopwatch, in a waterfront warehouse near Hamamatsucho.

The Publicity Working Group discreetly arranged media coverage for the event, Japan's first large-scale graffito, which would encompass a whole Chuo Line train.

The organization came to consider that ultimately the project had a bearing on national prestige, it being an opportunity to demonstrate to the world that Tokyo, too, was capable of producing public art as unstrung as the great work being done in the legendary American centers of urban intaglio—New York, Cleveland, and Detroit.

As the April 1 D-day approached, there was some concern that the organization had been infiltrated by the railroad police. A routine background check run by the Security Working Group on a member who had stated in his application that his job was parking bicycles at Nakano Station revealed that in fact he supported himself by dealing in counterfeit platform tickets. Fortunately for the project, this seemingly shady character turned out to be OK, if a trifle reckless.

The evening of March 31 was cloudless, with a soft mist lying near the ground. The tracks at the Mitaka holding yard, where most of the trains of the Chuo Line are bedded down overnight, glittered in the moonlight.

The surveillance team camped out on the benches on the platform at Mitaka Station, feigning a terrible weariness. This arrangement allowed them to keep the station personnel under observation at all times. If it chanced that the graffiti artists aroused suspicion, the surveillance team was to break out in a wobbly *enka* as a warning.

Painting began precisely at 3:45 A.M. It went like clockwork, without a hitch. By 4:15 the artists, all dressed in black like ninja, had withdrawn, taking their equipment with them.

The bleary-eyed train crew noticed nothing when they boarded the train at 5:55 A.M. The train pulled out of the yard at 6:15, bound for Tokyo. First stop was Kichijoji. As the train slid into the station, the commuters in their serried rows rubbed their eyes first in disbelief, then in delight.

The first five cars were painted like the cars of the Tohoku Shinkansen, and this modulated over the next several cars into a dragonlike design featuring great expanses of shimmering scales. A nymph stretched out the length of the next car, her head on a satin pillow, her hand holding an onigiri rice ball, as if for breakfast. Then a car painted to look like Halley's comet. The next several cars spelled out OHAYO GOZAIMASU and GANBARIMASHO in elegant lettering, and the last car was a psychedelic caboose, like a sixties album cover.

JR was not amused. Word went down the line and the anti-graffiti crew, which had been formed fifteen years ago but had never been called on, swung into action. They boarded the train at Nishi-Ogikubo armed with buckets of solvent and long-handled brushes. By Ochanomizu, the train was immaculate.

Walkman Wars

A recent letter to the editor of the *Spectator*, the eminent British weekly, runs:

> Sir: As I sit suffering in a British Rail train, a solution to the current trade deficit with Japan occurs to me. Surely British electronics can come up with a small device capable of jamming 'personal stereos' playing in one's vicinity. I predict a massive market. Yours faithfully, David Short, London.

The letter conjures up an image of an embattled Britain once again threatened with invasion by evil forces. Only a miracle weapon can fend the invaders off.

Let us say that Throgmorton Electronics, Ltd., rises to the challenge and comes up with the Throgmorton Zapper, a pocketable black box which, when Button A is pressed, will cause any Walkman-type mechanism within ten yards to run backward. The event will mark the beginning of what is sure to be known as the Walkman Wars.

Faced with the impending depersonalization of personal stereo, Walkman manufacturers will retaliate by fitting their latest models with an Anti-Zapper function capable of homing in on any Throgmorton Zapper in the vicinity and with a single pulse of a laser beam, melt it.

Throgmorton Electronics will then be forced to devise a device to zap the Anti-Zapper, and in this way the conflict will escalate.

It would only be a matter of time before Zapper technology would be applied to other electronic products which intrude on a tranquil urban existence. Encouraged by the commercial success of Throgzaps and their spinoffs, Japanese manufacturers would produce a device that would cause any *karaoke* apparatus within a half mile first to flat horribly, then to give out with a long, low Bronx cheer, then finally to burst into flames.

It would not be long before we would be able with the press of a button to dim all the neon in Shinjuku. Eventually Zapper-type devices would be available which would allow groggy commuters to adjust the volume of station-platform announcements, to reduce to a whisper the loudspeaker trucks of desperately electioneering politicians, and to sweetly modulate the jagged street jingles of Yodobashi Camera and other similarly public-spirited firms. Perhaps there would even be a device which would cause the carburetors of the motorcycles of night-riding *bosozoku* to clog up irredeemably.

In time, the market for Zapper-type devices would grow to be as large as that for the electronic equipment that constitutes their target, because few people would be willing to forego the control over their environment that the Zapper promised. People in public places would take to eyeing their neighbors suspiciously, and the government would propose that certain areas be posted ZAPPING PROHIBITED. Zappers would come to be worn on the wrist as an item of fashion, and cities around the world would be as quiet as the wind.

Too quiet, the first generation to grow up with the personal zapper is bound to think. This new generation would think of zappers as a silly old killjoy of an (English) invention, like automobiles with a partition between driver and passenger or eyeshades for nervous sleepers. Throgmortons would be outmoded, and collectors would pay antique shops stiff prices for classic models with fine detailing.

Tokyo would then once again become its noisy irrepressible self, just as before the wars. I suspect that deep down most people just as soon have it that way.

The Present Tyranny

It is curious that in a society as dedicated to sweetness and harmony as that of Japan, a tradition as potentially disruptive as the ritual giving of gifts has been allowed to flourish. People don't talk much about the consequences of indiscriminate gift giving for fear of being seen as mean, but it is clear that in Japan gifts are launched as missiles, serving, if rightly chosen, to stun the recipient, or as least to nudge him or her off balance.

As gift giving proliferates, it tends to be taken for granted, and so to achieve its purpose of impressing the other fellow with the giver's scarcely controllable generosity, the preferred gift has to be seen to be twice as magnificent as any sane person would deem reasonable.

In this way the ante escalates. If I give you a cheap souvenir teaspoon stamped "Shizuoka," you counterpunch with a packet of fine tea. I fight back with an antique teapot; you ambush me with a round trip for two to a luxury hotel on the grounds of a Sri Lankan tea plantation. I, panicking, present you with a one-third interest in Twinings . . . and so on until we are both bankrupt.

In Tokyo this annual escalation of gifts given takes place between companies who do business together: one company one year giving its client company ten cases of beer, the next twenty, the next forty, until all corridors, closets, washrooms, and space at the back of the recipient company's garage are filled with brightly wrapped packages from Mitsukoshi Department Store. At the end of the gift-giving season, the employees of both companies thus locked in gift-giving combat must hire trucks to cart away their share of the bounty, wanted or not, to their own homes and garages.

At a higher level, the presidents of the companies involved will exchange exquisite lacquer boxes, larger ones every year, each requiring the attention of a master craftsman for several months and costing millions of yen. It is said that the hills outside Kyoto are heavily populated with subtle geniuses whose sole occupation is the crafting of fine lacquer boxes destined to be presented by the heads of Japanese industry to each other during the two annual gift-giving seasons of *o-chugen* in the summer and *o-seibo* in the winter.

Escape from the gift-giving plague is impossible.

On every train platform, boxes of the local specialty—pickles, bean cakes, rice cakes, fish cakes, twirligigs—are dutifully purchased by travelers (although they may only have gone overnight to Osaka to visit an aged aunt) to be taken back and presented to fellow office workers and neighbors as a gesture of their enduring concern.

The constant flow of gifts keeps the Japanese economy purring and out in front of the unsupercharged economies of nations that don't indulge in frenzied gift giving. A good 15 percent of the revenue of the average department store is generated by gifts: boxes of bars of soap, cans of soup, tins of salad oil and pressed seaweed, matched bottles of wine and whiskey and 100-percent orange juice, and hampers of exotic foreign delicacies—a truly prodigious prodigality, as if to make up for the shameful thriftiness of the rest of the year.

Perhaps, though, this gift-giving reflex could be put to good use.

One hears that the American public continues to be concerned that they are buying more Japanese goods than Japanese consumers are buying American goods. Some Americans are evidently itchier than ever about the trade imbalance and have convinced themselves that behind it all there lurks some great brooding conspiracy.

Would not an appropriate gift serve to ease the tension? Why don't the Japanese people simply present the American people with a massive present, perhaps a video game or a motor scooter for everyone, or a new national railroad system (staffed by supernumerary JR railroad men), or maybe, because after all it is the thought that counts, an enormous lacquer box?

Scale of Crowdedness

It occurs to me that our ability to accommodate the urban ebb and flow would be greatly enhanced if we had a means to gauge the crowdedness of a situation with more precision than is now possible. Something like the Beaufort scale for the force of the wind or the Richter scale for earthquakes, for example, would be a useful descriptive tool.

If we had such a scale, people trying to decide whether to take the subway or Japan Railways would be able to consult their station's traffic board. A digital board would display the C.I. (Crowdedness Index) of each of Tokyo's subway and rail lines, and commuters could make their decision on how to travel accordingly, based on their ability to tolerate crunch.

I would like to propose the following logarithmic scale running from 1 (hardly crowded at all) to 7 (of a crowdedness not possible to exceed).

Level 1: Not more than seven people in view, the figure seven being drawn from an ancient Chinese manual of brush painting which holds that seven is the maximum number of anything which can be perceived at a glance as separate entities, anything over seven being perceived as vaguely numerous. This level of crowdedness occurs, for example, in rural situations during non-holidays, in private rooms in the city, and between one and five in the morning in the streets of the more circumspect Tokyo neighborhoods.

Level 2: At this level claustrophobics are susceptible to bouts of anxiety. While walking, you must adapt by ducking and bobbing like a halfback to the varying trajectories of others. When not walking, you will touch someone if you stretch your arms out. As, for example, in an elevator holding ten people.

Level 3: Ritual "*Sumimasens*" are heard to be uttered at a rate of at least six per minute. Arms pinned to side, briefcases clutched to breast. Angle of hat, if askew, not correctable. Shopping bag, if not juggled onto overhead rack, crushed. Situation perceived to be "crowded" by non-Tokyo residents.

Level 4: A body of people whose intention it is to be in motion cannot move at all for at least two minutes at a time, and when it does move, must shuffle collectively. As, for example, Meiji Shrine on January 1.

Level 4.5: At this level, it makes a difference what season of the year it is to those urban logisticians whose responsibility it is to calculate how many people can reasonably be expected to jam themselves into one car of the Yamanote Line: in winter, because people wear overcoats, the count is lower than in summer, so more trains must be scheduled.

Level 5: When people talk or gently hum along with their Walkman, those adjacent can feel the vibration of their vocal cords, and their bodies throb in sympathetic vibration. When people try to exit a railway car, 15 percent of them can expect one of the following to occur: watch torn off, coat button lost, shoe lost, glasses lost, hair or ear ornament lost, skirt twisted around back to front. Situation perceived to be "crowded" by Tokyo residents, who may even remark on it in a jocular way.

Level 6: A floating sensation: it is possible to lift your feet off the floor and be suspended in place. When the car door opens and passengers tumble out, the car can be seen to rise at least six inches on its springs.

Level 6.5: Ribs crack. Door windows set in rubber gaskets pop out.

Level 6.7: When people think, those adjacent can feel the vibrations of their brain waves. At this level, Buddhist holy men and Zen saints begin to swear and roll their eyes.

Level 7: Souls merge.

4. Some Tokyoites

Welcoming Speech

"Good morning, lady and gentlemen.

"I am Senior Managing Director Noguchi. I am happy to have the opportunity to welcome you here today and I hope you are not too much jet lag. Thank you for your spending your valuable time to come such a far distance to here to [*turns to read the long banner hanging behind him*] FIRST ANNUAL INTERNATIONAL MARUFUJI MEDIUM-HEAVY INDUSTRIES SALES AND MARKETING DISTRIBUTION TECHNOLOGY MANAGEMENT SEMINAR.

"The thema of this first annual international Marufuji medium-heavy, ah, seminar is how we can cooperate better in rapidly changing world environments. Concerning this, I hope you will relax yourself here in Tokyo and have many valuable discussions and exchanges of ideas. When you return to home please discuss these matters with key responsible persons on your side.

"By the way, we had terrible trouble last year with weak dollar, et cetera. The Marufuji companies all over the world experienced a rapidly changing market condition when the yen became strong suddenly. Our products might now be somewhat expensive! This calls for greater flexibility and heartfelt application from each and every one of us, all over the world.

"Changing the subject, I would like to take this opportunity to thank all members who worked so hard to install the new computer system. Now we have so many valuable informations about our sales

143

activities and many other things all over the world that it is necessary to hire various additional people in order to perform complete analysis. Now we know almost everything, which is very valuable, as you know.

"As for the last-month speech of President Hiramatsu outlining the new policy, new reorganization, new directions, new projects, and the new slogans and goals for the unique golden-opportunity decades in the near future, we at headquarters are totally committed to supporting all ideal new attractive trends with all our energy. A positive awareness of the necessary commitment is vital!

"Now I want to tell you some new important news. In order to contribute as much as possible to the trade balance, after a detailed study of various opportunities and the full support of various local officials, we have made the decision to construct a new crowbar factory in Elkins, Nebraska. This new production facility is scheduled to be on line next May, and we will need all of your usual cooperations to achieve it. We will supply the Canada, U.S., Mexico, and Central America crowbar markets by this plant, and we also plan to export crowbars from this plant to Japan. Too bad for our present crowbar plants in Kumamoto and Kawagoe, but they are too expensive. We will turn them into research facilities in some research area not decided yet. Perhaps sixth-generation computers might be of considerable interest.

"Many things will be presented the next three days, for example, the new products lineup, a review of this year's technical breakthroughs, and for your listening pleasure a candlelight concert by the Marufuji brass band.

"There will be time for questions and answers and arguing and heckling, which as you know is essential in order to understand each other well, because we are from all over the world.

"We are strong because we can communicate to each other our various experiences—our clever solutions as well as our silly little mistakes—by fax and by earnest conversation over green tea or, sometimes, whiskey.

"Maybe everything we say here is not so clear that you could exactly repeat it. Maybe sometimes you think we talk a little abstract. That's OK. We talk, you listen. You talk, we listen. When we have talked and listened enough, we will do something.

"Don't worry if this talking and listening seems to take much valuable time. Let us make our own schedules together. You will see, when we work together well, the schedule will easily decide itself. This is because no schedule is as important as the idea the schedule is about. When the idea is clear, the schedule is only detail.

"In this spirit of adventurousness—which I know you might think is a little crazy sometimes—we look into the future and plan together our growth in the 21st century.

"Thank you for taking your time to listen to me. I look forward to personally talking with each and every one of you at this evening's welcoming party."

Pachipro

Yoshio Kuwabara teaches people how to win at pachinko. He is a *pachipro*, a pachinko professional.

There was a time, Kuwabara says with no hint of boasting, when he could walk away a winner from any pachinko parlor in the country. But he is thirty-eight now, and his responsibilities as president of Cat's Time, the pachinko research organization he founded six years ago, have meant that he has little time to hone his skills on the current crop of machines (the ¥10 trillion industry introduces about one hundred new models each year), so he thinks that if he wanted to bankrupt a machine now he would first have to be briefed by his research staff.

Cat's Time's offices in Shin Okubo overflow with exotic electronic measuring devices and pachinko machines in various stages of dissection. Here the critical path of pachinko balls in new machines is analyzed with the aid of slow-motion video, and the program of their Read Only Memories is decoded with the aid of a computer. In the back room the staff practices on a bank of the newest machines, putting their theoretical strategies to the test. A stuffed crocodile hangs on the wall of the reception area, as if to demonstrate that any beast can be tamed, and scattered about are stacks of comics to feed the restless imagination of a staff whose average age is twenty-two.

Kuwabara sells the results of Cat's Time's research to the general public in books advising how to recognize a pachinko machine that is most likely to pay off, to subscribers in *Winning Pachinko*, a twenty-six-page monthly magazine which suggests strategic approaches to the season's new machines, and to about a thousand hardcore professionals who pay ¥50,000 a year to subscribe to an incredibly detailed series of analyses of new machines which have been determined to be vulnerable to specific stratagems. All three major manufacturers of pachinko machines subscribe to Cat's Time's publications because they provide valuable insights into the reason particular machines are popular with the pachinko-playing public.

The object of pachinko is to sneak a ball into a key slot in the center of the machine. When this is done, lights begin flashing, gongs begin clanging, and balls (which can be exchanged for prizes or, with some subterfuge, cash) begin pouring out of the machine. The machine is then said to have caught a "fever."

Kuwabara aims to instruct readers of his publications on how to infect a machine with fever. To do this they must first identify a hot machine. As an important factor in this is an assessment of the alignment of the nails on the face of the machine, Cat's Time's publications are filled with complicated diagrams showing how the balls will cascade when the nails are aligned in various ways, and calling attention to critical junctures. Kuwabara distributes to his clients a pocket gauge which allows the spacing between the nails to be quickly measured.

The world of pachinko is horrendously noisy, joyously gaudy, and is energized by comic-book fantasy, with machines with names like Bravo Jumbo, Prism Fighter, and Fever Miracle. Pachinko makes Tokyo the greatest gambling city in the world, with each of the city's 1,500 pachinko parlors supporting two or three pachipros who play the machines for a living. Yoshio Kuwabara is now an establishment figure in this world, and Cat's Time's publications are pachinko's *Wall Street Journal*.

Zokin

A young lady of our acquaintance named Riho Nukiyama, who has just entered the employ of a famous Japanese company, writes as follows.

"I suppose I had a slightly romantic idea of what it was like to work in a modern company. But I did know it would not be like the old days, when girls from good families did not go out into the world and work at all. In those days girls could never expect to have the same responsibility or authority as men.

"I had an idea—I think it must have come from an American film—that a modern working woman steps out of a cab with her tailored suit and Italian leather briefcase and hurries to a meeting to present her plan for the launch of an important new product in the North American market. In my dream, I would have that kind of responsibility. I would call my counterpart in New York once or twice a week to tell him how things were going in Tokyo, and he would call me sometimes to ask my advice. I would have the reputation of being very capable, and eventually I would be promoted to a position where I would be responsible for many people, many men and women.

"So I was very careful about choosing a company to work for. I wanted to avoid any company where women were thought somehow not capable of handling responsibility. I certainly wanted to avoid any company which hired women just to make copies, to serve tea, and to wipe the desks and clean the ashtrays every morning with a *zokin*, which is what we call a cleaning rag.

"So when I went for interviews in my dark suit, white blouse, and crimson ribbon around my neck, I tried to find out just how modern the company really was. They always asked me how serious I was, and I would always assure the people from Personnel that I would gladly work overtime and that I didn't mind working on weekends if I had to. I would smile to indicate my eagerness. *Of course* I would work as hard (or harder) than a male colleague. *Of course*.

"I was very happy when my company told me they would hire me. I talked to the girls working there and they seemed to love their work. To me, everything seemed wonderful and I was anxious to get started.

"Our first week was general training. Boys and girls both made speeches, had debates, played a management game, and went out to demonstrate various company products. People from a generation ago wouldn't have believed that girls would be given the same training as boys. But it was true! Not only were we given the same training, but we were being paid the same salary, and the company recognized that we had the same talent. I was so happy.

"After our week's general training we were assigned to the office where we would work. I went to my new office with a boy who was new, too. We were called into the meeting room and told we would be working together.

"We were given desks facing each other. While we were exchanging greetings with everyone in our new section, the lady office manager came over to my desk and placed a zokin on it. 'This is yours,' she said. 'You must help the other girls to wipe the desks in the morning and clean the ashtrays.'

"I stared at my zokin, not really knowing how to react. 'You should have known I was coming to you,' it seemed to say. Well, maybe so. I guess I wanted to hold on to my dream of 'equality' as long as I could.

"How do I feel now that I have seen the reality? It's all right. Just a little frustrating once in a while. It's easier to be friends with that little piece of cloth than disrupt the office and maybe make enemies. It's fine with me if ten minutes of work with my zokin every morning brings peace to the office. But still . . ."

The Fine Art of Name Calling

The lovers haven't seen each other for thirty years, but now she slowly approaches the mountain cottage where she has learned he lives alone. She fumbles with the latch of the gate, unsure of herself. He puts down his work and turns to face her, then, a split second before he freezes into the *mie* pose that a Kabuki actor assumes at the moment of peak emotion, there comes from the third balcony a cry of "Naritaya!" The cry is full-throated and supremely confident, and so masterfully timed that it serves to unite the audience of two thousand behind it and pitch the drama to an even higher level.

This calling out of the name of the school of an actor or some other phrase of encouragement is called *kakegoe* and is an old Kabuki tradition. Kakegoe is different in spirit from the "Look out behind you!" shrieked by the audience at an antique melodrama and different from the "Olé!" of enthusiastic afi-cionados at a bullfight because kakegoe is not spontaneous but calculated.

Kakegoe is not the whoop of the crowd but an individual effort requiring a sure knowledge of the play and the actors. While bad kakegoe does nothing more than call attention to the caller, good kakegoe has great style and augments the theatrical experience of everyone in the audience.

In Tokyo there are currently three kakegoe guilds, comprising about sixty members in all, all of whom have free passes to Kabukiza in recognition of their services to and participation in a performing art. Internecine squabbles about timing and protocol keep the guilds separate.

The current doyen of the kakegoe practitioners is a man named Mori. Now in his mid-eighties, Mori-san has eased away from his profession as house painter so that he can slip almost every day into a seat in the third balcony just over the *hanamichi*.

Mori-san is so assured in his technique that he has been known to leave his seat to beat the crowd to the exit as the performance draws to a close and turn as he makes his way up the aisle to let go a last salvo to skew precisely the final windup of tension of the whole three-hour program.

Actually, some practitioners of the kakegoe art maintain that it is not necessary to view the stage at all to know when to call. They call, they say, to the rhythm of the language.

A man named Mizutani, who died last year, was another great kakegoe artist. Mizutani-san was master of a sushi shop in Asakusabashi, but he would close the shop, often at the specific request of an actor's manager, in order to come to the theater to help to make a particular performance memorable.

Mizutani-san had a tremendous voice that resounded throughout the theater, and he would temper his tone to suit the occasion—a great booming call to an actor in the role of a warrior, a sweet and worshipful call to an actor playing a maiden.

His sense of timing was wondrous. In the play *Hiragana Seikuiki*, for example, at the grand entrance of Shigetada where others would key their call to the sound of the curtain being drawn back, Mizutani-san would roar out *"Mattemashita!"* ("We've been waiting for this!") just as the chanter chants ". . . Shigetada," after which there comes a thundering drum roll, and then the swish of the opening of the curtain.

Once when Mizutani-san became fed up with the petty politics of the guilds he went to Utaemon, one of the greatest of Kabuki actors, and told him that he was going to quit. "We cannot allow you to quit," Utaemon said. "You are too important to us."

Although some of the more conservative kakegoe practitioners hold that only third-generation *Edokko* are qualified to call out, in this era of social revolution when foreigners have become sushi chefs, geisha, and sumo wrestlers, the exclusiveness of the kakegoe guilds is being eroded. An Englishman named Ronald Cavaye is building a reputation for himself as a caller of talent. (Cavaye is a trained musician, which must help.) And now we are hearing well-timed calls from Suzuko Yoshizumi, who is not only the first woman to practice what has hitherto been an exclusively masculine endeavor, but is from the Kansai to boot.

Sunday in the Park
with the Gang

Last Friday was one of those sparkling days on the cusp of summer when you feel as gaga with contentment as a baby. I had no particularly pressing appointments, so I decided to indulge myself and spend the afternoon at the Ueno museum at the new exhibition of Chinese and Japanese art from the British Museum.

It turned out to be a wonderful exhibition, very well mounted. Some lovely lacquerware and porcelain, and there was a fantastic Chinese bronze pot with chubby gilt dragons for handles that just knocked me out. I spent three hours at the show and then I had to go.

Ueno Park was filled with high-school kids on their school trips and there were the usual slowly unraveling skeins of bus tourists being led through the hoops by their tour guides. I saw one tour group become accidentally merged with another and it took the two guides a good ten minutes of banner brandishing and exhortations to sort everyone out.

Then I noticed parked on the road two black Benzes flanking a silver-gray Cadillac with a wheelbase like a truck. All three cars were so highly polished they seemed spotlighted. Standing near the cars in a quasi-military formation was a group of about sixty men. They seemed to be waiting for a command.

The men on the outside of the phalanx were dressed casually in polo shirts and slacks. Some were wearing rubber zori, which contrasted strangely with their proud and very self-conscious bearing. In the middle of the group there were about twenty men with crew cuts and dark suits, and in the middle of them was a heavyset man in a suit modeled on that of a comic-book card shark, brown with wide electric-blue stripes. He seemed to be directing things out of the side of his mouth.

Then it came to me who they were. They were *yakuza*, Japanese gangsters.

Ever the curious bystander, I went up to one of them and asked as innocently as I could, "What are you doing?" He glowered at me through half-closed eyes but did not deign to answer.

I went around to the back of the group and asked again, "What are you all doing here, anyway?" "Nothing, *do not trouble yourself*," was the growl of an answer. These people were not going out of their way to make friends.

I think they must have been the top echelon of a major syndicate. They looked extremely tough, and I could not imagine why they had assembled there in Ueno Park on this fine day. Surely they had their rackets to attend to.

Then the fellow in the middle gave some sort of sign and the whole group began to move in a single file toward the museum. It occurred to me that they intended to plunder the treasures of the British Museum.

As they filed by, the last man turned to me and said, with a slight shrug of his shoulders, as if asking for my understanding of a very peculiar situation: "The boss wants to look at the art."

I wonder what the boss thought of the pot with the dragons.

Maintaining the Trains

Of all the wonderful strangenesses of Tokyo, even more eerie than the precision wrapping of presents and the cult of politeness is the otherworldly spotlessness of the city's trains. That Tokyo's trains should be the most crowded in the world and at the same time the cleanest suggests that something fanatical is at work.

You can run your hand along the outside of a Tokyo commuter train and chances are good that it will come away unbesmirched. This is not true of a New York commuter train, where sometimes you can't even see out of the window.

Last week I dropped in on Mr. Katsuyoshi Kandachi, chief of the Car Maintenance Division of the Toyoko Line, at his office in Motosumiyoshi to ask him how he does it. He introduced me to his three section chiefs and as we drank tea together at a table decorated with an arrangement of white chrysanthemums, he told me that the Toyoko Line has forty-six trains of eight cars each, for a total of 352 cars.

It is the duty of the train crew when the train reaches the end of the line, I learned, to check that all the lights work and that all newspapers and bottles and anything left behind by mistake are picked up. When the trains go off duty in the evening they are swept out and inspected for anything that needs immediate attention. Once or twice a year, for instance, someone sprays a furious graffito on the floor of a car; it is expunged the same night.

We went outside to look at the automatic washing

machine, sort of a giant car wash with eight nylon brushes as tall as a house, which each car is run through at least once every four days. We watched a train being washed. It went through the whirling brushes once with soap and water, then was run back and forth through geysers of water to rinse it off. Every eight days each car has its windows polished inside and out, its interior lights dusted off, its fan blades wiped clean, and the filter of its air conditioner changed.

Every twenty-eight days, each car is subjected to a cleaning shakedown which, as I saw, takes no shortcuts. After the train has been run through the washing machine, an outside crew of seven men in rubber boots, polished helmets, and long, purple dishwashing gloves washes the outside again by hand, using scrub brushes and polishing cloths, and a crew of fourteen women in yellow kerchiefs, blue sneakers, and long, purple dishwashing gloves cleans the interior of the cars in the following manner.

First, all the seats are removed and whatever passengers have managed to stuff down behind them—shortchange tickets, candy wrappers, advertising leaflets, wallets—is removed. The seats are then inspected for wear and soiling, then brushed and replaced. The luggage racks and the hanging straps—even the inside of the straps—and anywhere else a passenger can touch are dusted and polished. The foot plates between the cars are pulled up and the space underneath is vacuumed out. Spatulas are used to scrape chewing gum from the floor (gum and spilt cola are evidently the great scourges) and the floor is waxed and buffed. Lastly, a germicide is sprayed through the cars and an inspector goes through with white gloves like a drill sergeant. The whole process takes about three hours per train and when it is finished every car in the train looks as though it has just rolled out of the factory.

The train is then driven into a long shed for its monthly appointment with the white-gloved maintenance crew, which is divided into specialist teams. (Members of the maintenance crew spend six months in training before they are allowed to touch a train.)

Every bolt is tapped with a hammer to ensure its tightness and all equipment underneath the cars is wiped clean, after which an automatic machine called the "Dust Shooter" goes down a track alongside the train and vacuums the underside of the train. Fuse boxes and battery cases are opened and inspected and if necessary the wheels are trued. The maintenance crew changes into a new starched orange uniform at least every other day. Every tool has its place outlined on the wall and nobody goes home until every tool is back in its place (because a misplaced tool might cause damage).

I told Mr. Kandachi that his operation brought to mind a hospital. "It is a hospital," he said, "except that a hospital doesn't have to deal with that infernal chewing gum!"

Arubaito Diary

I have received the following communique from a sixteen-year-old American acquaintance who is fluent in Japanese and who, school being out, has just nailed down her first summer job:

"When I saw the sign in the window of Skylark, a chain restaurant, saying ARUBAITO, which means part-time job, I knew I had to move fast. There's a lot of competition for the good jobs. The last time I tried for a job I called to make an appointment but they never seemed to be free, so this time I went straight there.

"When I got there, a guy my age was being interviewed by the *tencho*, the boss. I could hear the questions. 'Why do you want to work?' 'How much money do you want?' 'What would you use it for?' Finally, the tencho said he would call if he got the job and the guy left with many bows and '*domos*.'

"I gave the tencho my resume. As he read he asked me a bunch of questions like 'How do you like Japan?' and 'Have you ever worked before?' He seemed pretty satisfied that I could answer in correct Japanese and he began to show interest in me as an American and asked about my father and my school. Then he told me he had decided to give me a chance, and he gave me a list of the meals, their nicknames, what tableware is used with each meal, and the prices. He said I was to memorize the list and come back in two days for a test."

The Test

"I walked into the office and was told to take a seat. I was given a list of all thirty meals and I had to write the price and tableware needed for each of them. At the bottom of the page were two extra questions: 'What would you do if a customer asked where the toilet was?' and 'What would you do if a customer asked for a cup of coffee?' I guess they wanted to know if you knew how to talk to a customer politely.

"I goofed on a couple of the prices but the tencho seemed fairly pleased. He doesn't show his emotions very much but the waitresses who were watching kept saying '*Sugoi!*' (Great!). I guess I passed.

"Then the tencho gave me a list of the ten basic polite expressions. He wasn't confident that an American would understand when to use each of these expressions but after mumbling to himself a bit he said, 'Let's try' and brought out a fifteen-minute video which showed how to talk to customers as well as the right and wrong way to wear the uniform. The video was very detailed and even showed how to hang the uniform up at the end of the day.

"When the video was over, the tencho gave me a form for my father to fill out giving his permission for me to work and told me to open a bank account by Monday, which would be my first day of work."

Monday

"When I walked in, I was greeted with a chorus of '*Ohayo gozaimasus*' (good morning). I thought this was strange as it was past four in the afternoon. It turns out that in a job like this, people greet each other this way when they see each other at the beginning of work, no matter what the time of day.

"I changed into my uniform and the tencho introduced me to Honma-san, my trainer. I was to follow her around and watch her. Each time a customer came in I was to say '*Irasshaimase!*' (Welcome!). At first I wasn't loud enough and the tencho would look at me and shout out a better example.

"By the second hour I was giving new customers their *oshibori* and glasses of water. Each glass of water had to have three ice cubes in it and be seven-eighths full. To place a glass on the table it had to be held a third of the way from the bottom and your pinky used as a cushion so the glass could be put down without making a sound. To refill a cup of coffee, you should say '*Shitsurei shimasu*' (Excuse me), pick up the cup, take one step backward, pour the coffee, and place it noiselessly back on the table so that the cup's handle is on the customer's left, then say '*Shitsurei shimasu*' again and maybe knock off a little bow if you have time."

Tuesday
"On my second day I was scheduled to work for three hours. The tencho was off so all the waitresses were happy.

"At first I did just what I did the day before: bringing oshibori and water, refilling coffee cups, and cleaning up. But then a lot of people came in all at once and everyone got so busy no one could tell me what to do. I did what I thought I should, but when I went to one table to do my oshibori and water thing I realized that I couldn't escape before they started to order and no one would be able to come to help me.

"They ordered all at once and then began to cancel and reorder and I couldn't keep up because I wasn't familiar with how to write the order in the proper way. It was chaos, and the customers were getting impatient. Finally, another waitress came over and straightened everything out, thank God.

"After that I was *scared* to take orders. I told everyone about the incident and they sympathized with me but the tencho, who came in later that day, just asked how the customers had reacted and gave me a copy of the menu to memorize that evening."

Wednesday
"By the time I reported for work I had the menu

down pat and that gave me confidence. Today was just the tencho and me, bad news. Every time I gave a customer water or something he'd be looking over my shoulder and after I finished he would correct my mistakes, like putting the glass on the table so you could hear it hit. He even corrected my walking, which he said was too American.

"Anyway, he seemed to be pretty satisfied because he didn't get *mad* at me."

Thursday

"Today everything went well. It was just the tencho and me again until four girls came in for the evening rush. The tencho took me aside for another video, this one about how to do *chukan-sage*, which means taking away the dishes before dessert. The key thing is timing. It can't be too early and it can't be too late. You have to watch carefully.

"After the video the tencho tested me on how to take orders. I passed with no mistake, which I think disappointed him because he just loves to correct us. Then he asked me to serve him coffee and I made a mistake with the spoon, but I guess I passed.

"Anyway, he let me go back to work because the rush had begun. I took the order of a couple and at the end of their meal they complimented me by saying they couldn't tell I was American because I spoke so naturally.

"I felt really good. Then I broke a wine glass by trying to work too quickly, but everyone said don't worry, it happens sometimes.

"Toward the end of my shift I felt bouncy and cheerful and customers started to ask me questions like 'Are you American?' and 'Do you like Japan?'

"Anyway, I'm having fun."

5. The Devil's Language

Japanese in One Easy Lesson

The burgeoning enrollments of Japanese-language schools here and, by all accounts, just about everywhere else suggest that the word has gotten around that, contrary to popular myth, Japanese is a learnable language and that certain cultural and commercial benefits can accrue if one is able to enter into the conversations that regularly take place in this country in that language. Evidently vast chunks of time and money are being spent by foreigners in an effort to commit to memory the most basic two thousand *kanji*, the most common polite verbs, and the proper way to count birds, boats, and chests of drawers.

Someone should tell these earnest learners that the similarity between Japanese and other languages is illusory. Japanese is not a medium of communication in the ordinary sense of that phrase. Foreigners' failure to realize this is why the Japanese they speak sounds so much like Spanish or Bulgarian transposed into a Japanese vocabulary.

When people speak Japanese to each other they are most of the time doing nothing more than reaching out as fellow human beings, fellow *Japanese* human beings, and assuring each other that the world's basically all right even if it is very hot (cold) today isn't it? This is why there are so many phrases in Japanese—like *atsui desu ne*—that carry nothing a foreigner would recognize as meaningful content. These phrases are like the first notes of a duet and act as an invitation to the person being addressed to join in for a quick warble before going on about their business.

If you doubt what I say is true, then ask yourself why it is that even Japanese of considerable sophistication have such a wretched time writing a simple, well-organized exposition in English. They can't do it, and the reason is *they never do it in Japanese*.

With the above as background, you are now ready for your lesson in essential Japanese. As I make it, you need only ten words and phrases to carry you gracefully through just about any situation. With such a limited vocabulary, you will not be able to impress others with your verbal wizardry, of course, but this is not only unnecessary, it is unadvisable. In Japan it is simply bad form to try to make an impression with fancy flights of language. That is what foreigners are always trying to do in all those other languages.

The first phrase to learn is *yoroshiku onegai itashimasu*, or simply, with people you know reasonably well, *yoroshiku*. English translations of this phrase are invariably grotesque—something like "I ask you to look favorably on me"—but it can be used to mean almost anything from "Hello" and "Goodbye" to "Please lend me ¥10,000" and "Don't bother me." It is very polite, which means that it snaps everyone to attention and has the effect of bringing any conversation to a halt.

Because conversations in Japanese are never between people of equal social status (people of equal social status tend to be friends and can therefore dispense with conversation altogether), they generally take the form of the superior recounting his view of the world to the inferior. In this case, as the inferior (you are the inferior, just take my word for it and don't worry about it), you must know how to keep the conversational ball rolling.

You do this by interspersing at roughly ten-second intervals either *Naruhodo* ("Naturally") or *So desu ne* ("Why didn't I think of that?"). If in the course of the conversation you should be asked for your opinion you merely cock your head and say *saaa*, which means "That's an extremely provocative question and there's really no way an ignoramus like me could even begin to answer it."

When someone makes you a proposition, your answer is *maaa*, followed by the sucking in of enough air to mimic the sound of a leaky balloon. The range of meanings thus conveyed runs from "That would be nice" to "That would be nice but it's impossible" to "That's an outrageous suggestion," depending on the amount of air sucked in.

If the conversation is very long and your interlocutor is explaining something difficult and involved, as for instance how to use the phone book, you can give the impression of following the explanation perfectly if at the end of every other sentence you nod your head and say either *ahh, ehh, umm,* or *haa,* all uttered with a short explosive puff of air, something like a hiccup.

If you would like any part of the explanation run by you again, all you have to say is *sooo?* with a rising inflection and raised eyebrows. As people here are very used to having to explain things twice or three times, your *sooo?* will not reveal that you have only been able to grasp the barest outline of what's been going on.

Finally, there's *yappari* (sometimes, for variety, *yahari*), which, when used in response to any statement by the other fellow, even the most innocuous, serves to suggest that your view of the world is on a higher plane than his. For example:

Other fellow: "The paper says it won't rain tomorrow."

You: "Yappari." (Meaning "Well of course they would, given their limited experience, but anyone with any sense at all can see that we're in for a typhoon.")

That's it. Lots of Japanese limit themselves for days at a time to this short vocabulary and seem none the worse for it. The thing is, you as a foreigner must put aside your urge to explicate, to explain, to comment on everything in sight. In Japan, silence is a perfectly valid mode of social intercourse and anyone who talks a great deal just gives the impression of bubbleheaded arrogance.

On Being Illiterate

I have tried to learn how to read Japanese, but I have been routed. A miserable residue of my efforts remains. I can decipher a couple of hundred *kanji*— "foot," "mouth," "river," "fish," "house," "mountain," "love"—and maybe another hundred or so more look reasonably familiar (doesn't count, I know), but all that is to reading Japanese as being familiar with the alphabet is to reading English. I am illiterate. Oh, the shame of it.

Actually, I have lived in Tokyo long enough that my illiteracy doesn't bother me anymore. I have risen above it. I survive. I remember or can puzzle out most place names after I've been there once or twice—I can get Okurayama from the "Oh" and the "yama," for example, and I recognize the kanji for "Danger," "Warning," and "No Entrance," although it helps if they are written in red at the top of a notice. I can read "No Smoking" and "The next train has left the previous station."

With a bit of luck, I can pronounce the name of someone who gives me his business card, but when I manage to pull this little parlor trick off I feel like an amateur magician with only one trick in his repertoire, because that is as far as it goes. Unless by chance, the fellow works at Hitachi. I can read "Hitachi."

Every morning, over the shoulders of fellow commuters, I scan the newspaper headlines for the news of the day. I can make out that something has happened to someone called Takeshita. The Giants have either won or lost by 3–2. It appears that three people were killed somewhere in some sort of an accident. It's my morning crossword puzzle.

I can read anything in *kana*, for what it's worth. It's not worth much. It's like being able to read all the crazy advertising slogans in the world but nothing else. It also means I can read the last couple of syllables of verbs, which is, of course, useless.

When I attend an elegant reception and am asked to brush-write my name in the book I can do so, but it looks as though it's been written by a five-year-old. I have to resist thinking that foreigners who can write their own name with something resembling confidence are terrible showoffs.

I study the ads in the train, hoping for the tiny thrill that comes when a phrase clicks. Sometimes a wonderful thing happens and I can read a *whole sentence.* It doesn't even bother me when the sentence turns out to be something like, "You and me and the wind—summer in Kyushu."

Of course the advertisements for just-published magazines use a lot of English words which I can easily make out. Although they cannot be trying to convince me personally to buy their magazine, I notice the word "SEX" in Roman letters appears an awful lot in these ads. Is there no Japanese word for sex? Perhaps they don't want young kids to buy their magazine.

Sometimes I have to leave someone a note. After ten minutes of mental hard labor I might be able to get out, "You are late. Meet me there. Riku." But will my friend be able to read it?

I remember receiving a long letter from a girlfriend. I went through it kanji by kanji for a hint to its general drift. After a certain amount of agonizing, I finally showed it to a friend, hoping that it wasn't too intimate, and asked for it to be read to me. It turned out that she had invited me to go flower-viewing with her, but by the time I had gotten it all figured out the blossoms had fallen.

I keep telling myself that it's OK. Japanese is a very difficult language. But then how did my daughter get it all down in a couple of years of intermittent study? It's embarrassing to have to ask your daughter to read you your mail and *I'm not going to put up with it anymore*!

I have just resolved to start carrying around with me again, just as I used to in more innocent times, a card printed with a kanji, showing the order of the strokes and giving three or four words in which the kanji is used. I'll study my kanji card while I wait for the train. This one I've got today looks pretty interesting: AKU, evil, *o, waru* (*i*), *a* (*shi*), bad, wrong, *waru,* a villain, *niku* (*i*), hateful (as second component) difficult to, *niku* (*mu*), to hate. It's only eleven strokes. I ought to have it down pat in a week or two. That is, if it doesn't get used as a bookmark before then.

The Secret Language of T-Shirts

Visitors to Tokyo perceive the English which decorates our T-shirts and shopping bags and subway posters as mangled, because it doesn't say what they expect. As they read these elliptical phrases, they experience the sensation of being on a train which has rocketed off its rails.

Actually, these mysterious words and snatches of semisentences convey exactly the meaning the writer wishes. They display a kind of folk wisdom, albeit filtered through an unfamiliar vocabulary and grammar. If you think of these phrases as found poetry, you will be richly rewarded. There is a rightness to them, if you give them a chance.

ZEITGEIST splayed across the front of a T-shirt cannot be merely the celebration of a modish literary word. It is surely a jab at the whole idea of printing slogans across our chests, a phenomenon of our bumpersticker times. RELAX ZONE and OPTICAL ILLUSION across the chest of a young lady are quite obviously in the same tongue-in-cheek spirit.

A very large woman weaves by on a pedal tricycle. On her bright yellow T-shirt a single word: ESPECIALLY. Exactly!

A young lad with a haircut inspired by *Grease* swaggers down the platform. On the back of his jacket he announces his affiliation: BULLIES.

A subway poster commissioned by a manufacturer of audio equipment who senses that the public is uncomfortable with the new technology shows a lady with liquid eyes in a cashmere sweater gazing longingly at a stereo system. The poster is headed ROXY DIGITAL AND HUMANITY. Impossible to put it more succinctly.

On the back of a jacket worn by a sweet young thing: BURN WITH LOVE. KISS. YOU MAY WELL SAY SO. The dying fall is worthy of an Elizabethan love sonnet.

What better description of a series of romantic paperback novels than *Heart Cocktails*? What more engaging description of *Comic Burger* (itself a brilliant name for easily consumable literature), a new comic magazine featuring tough guys as heroes, than *Hardboiled Wonderland*? What cozier name for a bridal advisory service than *Wedding Mama*? What more to-the-point description of a hairdresser than *Ego Mechanic*? The label on a denim workshirt says ANCIENT BRITISH SENTIMENT, economically evoking images of traction engines and the upper-class sweat required to build an empire. MEAL, COMBAT, INDIVIDUAL. TURKEY OR CHICKEN, BONED on the back of a jacket would seem to be an American version of the same thing.

On the belt of a svelte lady: 1982 LIGHT MENU. A resolution hewn to, evidently, and worth announcing.

On a shopping bag: IF. If I were a rich man. . . . Should we not initiate the annual burning into a slope on the outskirts of Kyoto the potent rune IF?

Sometimes these phrases are earnest admonitions, a common mode of expression in Japan. Thus, on a cap: WILDERNESS BY ESCAPE. LET US FIND SOMETHING THAT MAY BE IMPORTANT FOR US. Good advice in the form of a cri de coeur. Or on a rucksack: I INSIST THAT YOUNG MEN MUST BE COSMIC BEFORE THEY CAN BE COUNTRY. Must keep our priorities straight. Or more loosely, on a denim jacket: FRAIS ESPECE. FORMIDABLE THE RISING EAR. BE INDIGNANT. PERPLEXITY. BE AMAZED. In other, more prosaic, words, don't settle for the easy shot. Be indignant, indeed. Do not go gentle.

On the back of still another jacket: SUPERJOCKS. WE ARE SEEING ENDLESS DREAMS. WE ARE LIKELY TO BE AT A STANDSTILL. BUT, CERTAINLY, WE WILL COME INTO NOTICE ALL OVER THE WORLD. ESTABLISHED 1986. This is the most poignant statement of youthful yearning I have ever come across.

I like, too, the giddy parrot on a T-shirt from whose beak comes the single word WHOM, thus neatly putting paid to Poe. And the winsome paean to nonconformity expressed by the phrase FREAKISH APPLESEED embroidered so matter-of-factly over a pocket stuffed with pens.

But perhaps the finest apercu of all is this program synopsis in English of a play called *Heartland* which had a short run in Shinjuku a while back: "*Heartland* is a very strange place and has very very strange peoples in it. Every day they play tennis at day and at night 'heaven-hell' game. Then big whales come to join them." My experience exactly.

Language, Schmanguage

In his jaunty book *Whereabouts: Notes on Being a Foreigner*, Alastair Reid writes, "To alight in a country without knowing a word of the language is a worthwhile lesson. One is reduced, whatever identity or distinction one has achieved elsewhere, to the level of a near-idiot, trying to conjure up a bed in sign language. Instead of eavesdropping drowsily, one is forced to look at the eyes, the gestures, the intent behind the words. One is forced back to a watchful silence."

Well, yes. If you don't know the language it is very difficult to hold up your end of the conversation, but it is absurd to be intimidated by this, absurd to feel an idiot, because the babble you happen to be comfortable with is different from the other fellow's babble. It makes as much sense as feeling embarrassed because your electric razor runs on a different voltage than that of the local power supply.

There are, of course, a number of fairly crude ways of relieving any embarrassment you might have at not happening to be conversant in the language of your neighbors. Stephen Potter (of *Gamesmanship*, you remember) recommended action in a situation of similar dynamics: when your doctor asks you to take off all you clothes except your socks you feel silly, so the doctor is in a transcendent position. Your counter-strategy is to arrange for a friend to telephone the doctor's office and ask for you. When you get the telephone, proceed to hold an extended, obviously highly enjoyable conversation with your friend, frequently slapping your naked thigh in delight. The longer the conversation goes on, the more uncomfortable the doctor will become.

Some other sage of social interaction once advised what to do if you find yourself intimidated by an imperious maitre d'hotel in a high-class Paris restaurant. *Whatever you do don't attempt to speak French.* Make your desires known in rapid and highly idiomatic English or, better, Flemish. It should be noted, however, that this strategy has the disadvantage of alienating you forever from the maitre d'.

In this country, there is no need to resort to such brutal tactics when confronted with the alien language called Japanese. For cultural reasons, bluster will get you less than nowhere. It is far better to rest easy, to communicate only with an occasional friendly nod or even a shrug to indicate that, while you are hopelessly lost, you are not concerned because it is obvious to you that the company you find yourself in is wonderfully congenial.

This works both ways. I recall when I first arrived in Tokyo spending an evening touring the local drinking establishments with a Japanese acquaintance whose only English was the phrase "the infinitely wise United States Constitution." At that time my only Japanese was *hidari, migi,* and *massugu,* words essential for communicating with taxi drivers. Although I suppose we had no great meeting of minds that evening, my friend and I probed the depths of political philosophy with gesture, smirk, and guffaw and had a fine time.

I am convinced that it is possible for a foreigner to go into any Japanese restaurant and *without uttering a word* cause a meal to be brought forth. (Beside this, conjuring up a bed is child's play.) If in a Japanese restaurant you should feel, in Alastair Reid's phrase, "reduced to the level of a near-idiot," you will only cause confusion and painful, painful commiseration, besides which you will very probably get nothing to eat. What you must do is sit down, put some money on the table in an unobtrusive way, and with a smile on your face swirl a hand in the air. I guarantee that you will eat well.

Actually, it is easier to communicate (that is, be part of what's going on) without language in Japan than any other place in the world, because the Japanese themselves mistrust language (that's why there are so many set phrases in Japanese), and also because in Japan it's perfectly all right in any social situation to say nothing at all, to just be there.

One's "identity or level of distinction" pretty obviously has nothing to do with one's ability to communicate across a language barrier. It takes only a quiet confidence in oneself and a certain sense of fun. Think of it as a charade, with the whole world taking part.

How Vagueness Spurs Creativity

My friend Tanaka is convinced that it is possible to build a machine capable of translating English into Japanese and vice versa. He tells me that there is already a machine that can turn English into reasonably intelligible Japanese, but that to go the other way and turn Japanese into English is a much, much harder nut to crack. To translate Japanese into English takes ten times the computer time and the results are often exceedingly bizarre. Whereas the English sentence has an internal logic to it—subject, verb, object—so it is something like a ladder with its rungs all in place, built for a purpose, *going somewhere*, the Japanese sentence, if it is even a sentence at all in the English sense, is more like a cloud in the sky, to which great billowy emendations can be made at any point.

Here, for example, is a typical Japanese sentence transposed with dogged faithfulness into English: "As far as the time is concerned I'm all right, but Suzuki sometimes has things to do and..." Brutalized into meaningful English, this would come out: "Suzuki is not dependable."

It is a mistake to conclude from this, however, that the Japanese language is somehow flawed. In fact, Japanese is perfectly suited to its purpose, which is to be a medium of easy social communication. Japanese positively *resists* precision, because precision can lay the foundation for confrontation. This is why there are no courses teaching writing at any Japanese university. It is also why Japanese companies, when they want to avoid the possibility of misunderstanding in a formal communication between themselves, will often resort to English, because straining for precision in Japanese is awkward and sounds like hectoring. The crux of it is that while English speakers are uneasy with imprecision, Japanese speakers are equally uneasy with precision. Computers, of course, are no good at dealing with imprecision—the switch is either on or off.

In Tokyo pubs in the evening, lofty metaphysical discussions are as rare as solitary drinkers. The Japanese rarely experience the urge to speculate that is apt to come over speakers of languages more insistent on logic. Japanese everyday communication already contains a sufficiently large speculative component to satisfy even the most rabid itch to engage in metaphysical wordplay. It is not surprising, therefore, that the Japanese religious impulse is firmly rooted in the here and now and that political discourse which seriously wrestles with abstractions is in this country almost nonexistent.

The result of this draining off of the creative energy that would otherwise go into philosophizing is that the Japanese have an intensely practical interest in the world around them. The natural creativity of the Japanese is not evidenced in the construction of new systems of thought, but in the devising of new *things*.

The Western model of a creative person is the artist alone in his studio or the solitary inventor working late in his lab. In Japan, things get invented by someone (afterward, no one can remember who) throwing out an almost offhand suggestion, and the suggestion's being refined by everyone chipping away at it from all angles, turning it over and over, critiquing it again and again until it emerges, perhaps years later, as a product, Mark I. The Japanese public then subjects the product to its own ruthless critique, and in time Mark II, an improved model, is produced.

While the Westerner's creative juices flow most freely and nobly when his is grappling verbally with ideas, the Japanese are most truly creative when working together on a concrete physical problem, such as how some mechanism can best be made to work. To sit in on an eighteen-hour-long study session attended by Japanese engineers engaged in a search for the solution to a complex technical problem is a revelation. Afterward, the blackboard looks like a chart of the theological system of St. Thomas Aquinas. In Japan, such a discussion is the equivalent of metaphysical speculation.

Japanese as a New World Language

William Safire, who writes a column about language and other contentious matters for the *New York Times*, tells of a telex he received from a Professor Burt Weeks of Syracuse University which read "Pls use yr consid influence to advse tv netwks that Tokyo has only two syllables instead of To-key-oh."

Safire telexed back "Tokyo is three syllables in NBC Handbk of Prnunciashun so stik consid influence in yr ear." The English-speaking world, snorted Safire in conclusion, has adopted the three-syllable usage, and that's the way it is.

Well, yes. I suppose so. But setting aside the short-circuited spelling of this exchange for the moment, surely it is arrogant of English as a language with a huge international following to play so fast and loose with the set of syllables a world city uses to refer to itself. Actually, English seems to have a particular genius for corrupting foreign place names—"Cologne," "Moscow," "The Hague," "Florence," and "Munich" are all inventions of the English tongue. The Japanese language, although *katakana* allows only a rough approximation of foreign place names, still comes closer than English to the local pronunciation: "Kerun," "Mosukuwa," "Hagu," "Firense," and "Myunhen."

One wonders, could Japanese ever replace English as the No. 1 international language. It's not impossible.

Japanese seems already to be nibbling away at the ascendancy of English. Courses in Japanese are being instituted in schools and universities around the world at a far higher rate than any other language and there is evidence that these courses are attracting the brightest and most diligent students.

This great interest in Japanese is pretty obviously fueled by this country's economic performance. Learn Japanese and get a High-Paying Job, is the idea. But we know that once a language has managed to establish a solid power base, as Spanish did in the fifteenth and sixteenth centuries, as French did in the eighteenth century, and as English did in the nineteenth, then given the right conditions it can spread rapidly through a kind of linguistic imperialism.

English, the competition, is in some disarray at the moment. There is considerable dialectical infighting—large chunks of both coasts of the United States are now Spanish-speaking, and Indian English, Philippine English, and Bronx English are mutually unintelligible. In an age of nationalism, many non–English-speaking countries are a good deal less enthusiastic about the teaching of English than in palmier days. In addition, to the extent that a language's hegemony depends on a solid economic and political base, the faltering industry and increasingly bizarre political adventures of the English-speaking nations provide a shaky base for continuing influence.

It used to be said that the two fundamental reasons for the preeminence of English were that the language had such a rich vocabulary (lifted from Latin, Greek, French, German, and any other language that had a likely jewel), and that the science of the English-speaking world was so advanced that if you wanted to take part in the scientific dialogue you had to know English because all the hot scientific words were English.

Neither of these distinguishing characteristics carries much weight anymore. Japanese is a far more acquisitive language than English ever was, vacuuming up concepts from all the world's languages and contorting them to its own needs, and now Japanese science and technology is itself coining new scientific words and acronyms at such a rate that a Japanese jargon jungle almost as thick as that of English has resulted.

Some will insist that Japanese can never become a world language because Japan has an alien, inward-directed culture, and besides, who could ever learn to write those squiggles? These are outmoded arguments.

First, Japan is no longer an alien culture. A country with the largest automobile industry in the world, the highest per capita newspaper circulation, the highest longevity, the most competitive educational system, and the lowest crime rate can only be said to be an alien culture if you suppose that these are not useful goals for any society to aspire to.

As for the squiggles, they are less a barrier to Japanese becoming widely used if you consider that it isn't primarily at the literary level that a language takes hold across linguistic boundaries. The crazy orthography of English was certainly no great barrier to English assuming its current role as No. 1.

What counts is whether or not the language can

be used to transact everyday business: to scold the neighbor's children, to argue with the butcher, to ask the way to the post office. Latin maintained its supremacy as a written language well into the Middle Ages, while all around it there swarmed the new languages of the streets. I foresee a situation in which English could continue to maintain its position as the language of case law, of pithy editorials in newspapers of record, and of elevated academic discourse, while Japanese, with its simple grammar, simple pronunciation, and fund of cheery set phrases, takes over as the world's vernacular.

Besides, we now have word processors that can write *kanji* for us, what little we are called on to write anymore. In Japanese offices, where the vaunted Japanese style of management presumably holds sway, very little is committed to paper. The bulk of mass communication is now advertising, and if it comes to that, any sane person would prefer to live with the elliptical, low-key advertising style which seems particularly suited to the Japanese language rather than the boastful stridency of too much of English-language advertising. English may well talk itself to death!

Of course, all this is only wild speculation. What will more likely happen is that the new world language will be an amalgam of English and Japanese, with odd bits of topical slang thrown in, an eternally shifting middle ground between the languages of the world's first and second economic powers.

GLOSSARY

Visitors to Japan soon come into contact with words and phrases which everyone, Japanese and foreigners alike, use to describe the Japanese experience. The essays in this book perforce include a lot of this vocabulary, the meaning of which I have tried to make clear here. In effect, this is a short course in how to talk like an Old Japan Hand.

aizuchi
> The aizuchi lady on TV is the lady who keeps nodding and saying "yes, yes" and "good point!" while her (male) counterpart rambles on.

Akihabara
> Tokyo's electrical-goods sales district, a madhouse.

arubaito
> Part-time work, from the German *arbeit*.

asagaoichi
> "Morning-glory market" held every July, at which hundreds of amateur horticulturists gather to offer for sale thousands of pots of morning glories they have raised. Definitely the place to buy your morning glories.

"Atsui desu ne?"
> "It's hot, isn't it?"

bento
> Boxed lunch of rice, fish, pickles, etc. Cheap bento are available at most railway stations while more elaborate ones made to order by specialist restaurants make the basis of a fine picnic.

Bon
> The time of the year, in August, when the ancestors are remembered. Most of Tokyo leaves the city to return to their *"furusato,"* their hometown; therefore, a good time to visit Tokyo.

bosozoku
> Motorcycle gangs who love to practice revving their machines *en masse* at two o'clock in the morning.

Boys' Festival
> May 5, also known as *Kodomo no hi*, during which boys are urged to be tough and never give up.

bucho
> "Division Chief," a step above *kacho*.

Calpis
> A soft drink unique to Japan, based on fermented milk. Not bad, actually.

Chiba
> The peninsula bordering Tokyo Bay to the east. Although Chiba has some lovely landscapes, Tokyo people insist on thinking of it as impossibly backward and dull—Tokyo's New Jersey. A good place to live if you don't have to come into the city every day.

chindonya
> The onomatopoetic word for a street band which hires itself out to draw attention to the opening of a new store, pachinko parlor, etc.

"*Chirigami kokan de gozaimasu.*"
> "This is the waste-paper exchange man." The call of the waste-paper collectors who drive from neighborhood to neighborhood on their collection run. They will give you a roll or two of toilet paper in exchange for your old newspapers and magazines.

chorei
> Meeting at the beginning of the working day to make sure that everyone knows what's happening, even if *nothing's* happening.

Chuo Line
> The main railway line from Shinjuku out through the western suburbs.

Dolls' Festival
> March 3, *Hina Matsuri* or Girls' Day.

domo
> "Thanks."

donburi
  A bowl of rice with something on top, for instance a fried pork cutlet (*katsudon*) or an egg and slices of chicken (*oyako donburi*).

Edokko
  "Child of Edo," Edo being the old name for Tokyo. Traditionally a Tokyoite with at least two generations of antecedents born in *shitamachi*, Tokyo's old downtown.

enka
  Japanese folksongs, or modern songs in that style, which are characterized by an overwhelming poignancy.

furoshiki
  A cloth used to wrap objects to be carried—in effect, a collapsible suitcase.

ganbarimasho
  "Let's go for it!"

Genroku-zushi
  A chain of sushi shops famous for its cheap prices, achievable because the sushi parades past the customers on a conveyor belt allowing them to grab what strikes their fancy.

geta
  Wooden clogs. Footgear worn with *yukata*.

Golden Bat
  A cheap cigarette with strong rural connotations, like Bull Durham, say.

hachimaki
  Twisted towel worn around the head to keep sweat out of the eyes and to indicate to everyone that the wearer is *determined*.

hanamichi
  A ramp running from the stage to the back of the theater. Sometimes used for entrance and exit of actors.

hanko
  One's personal seal.

hidari
  "To the left."

hinoki
Japanese cyprus, a sensuous wood.
hiragana
See katakana.

ikura
Salmon roe. Delicious stuff.
irasshaimase
"Welcome!"
isshobin
The magnum-sized bottle classic sakés come in.

jinrikisha
A rickshaw. Now only used by geisha to move in style from one engagement to another. Of an evening, you can spot them in Tsukiji, for example.
JR
Japan Railways

kacho
"Section Chief," the first rung on the corporate ladder.
kaiseki
The most elegant (and most expensive) mode of Japanese cooking, inspired by the tea ceremony.
Kamakura
The ancient capital, an hour's train ride from Tokyo Station. Although infested with writers and politicians, it remains a charming town.
kamishibaiya
Old-time storyteller, who would wheel his bicycle into a neighborhood and engage a crowd of kids with his storytelling, after which he would sell them candy.
kana
Hiragana and *katakana* taken together.
kanji
The Chinese characters. Everyone has to learn upwards of two thousand kanji before they can graduate from high school and that's why not much work gets done at a Japanese university—everyone is exhausted.

Kansai
> The area of Japan in which Osaka is the major city, as opposed to the Kanto area, in which Tokyo is the major city.

karaoke
> A plague. The gruesome spectacle of someone without an ounce of talent blearily crooning into a microphone the lyrics of old Sinatra songs to a recorded orchestral accompaniment. Most often encountered in saké pubs fairly far along in the evening, to the discomfort of the neighbors.

katakana
> The Japanese syllabary used mostly for foreign words, as opposed to *hiragana*, the Japanese syllabary used for Japanese words. It is as if when a French word appeared in a passage of English prose, a completely different alphabet were used to represent it.

katsudon
> A fried pork cutlet on top of a bowl of rice.

Kawasaki
> An industrial wasteland between Tokyo and Yokohama.

kiosk
> Stands at railway stations selling newspapers, magazines, souvenirs, beer, cups of saké, toys, cheap reading glasses, and God knows what else.

koban
> The neighborhood police box.

kokeshi
> Wooden doll indigenous to the rural communities of northern Japan. It is said that these dolls were originally carved as a remembrance of the babies which poor farming families were forced to eliminate, as they didn't have enough food to feed them. Kokeshi are now sold as craft artifacts.

konnichiwa
> "Hello."

kotatsu
> Take a low table, install a heating mechanism under it, drape a covering over it, and you have a warm place to snuggle when the weather turns chilly. In the winter, everyone in the house gravitates to the kotatsu, which may be why Japanese families are so close.

massugu
"Straight ahead."

mazegohan
Rice mixed with fried tofu, vegetables, etc.

meishi
Business card. Don't leave home without it.

mie
A dramatic pose struck in Kabuki.

migi
"To the right."

mikan
A Japanese fruit which recalls the tangerine.

monpei
Baggy cotton trousers worn by farm wives.

nijikai
After the formal party adjourns, those still in the mood continue at a more informal nijikai—a "second party."

Nikkei-Dow
The Japanese Dow-Jones.

ninja
Dressed all in black, ninja are masters of the martial arts. They know how to make themselves invisible and how to leap buildings at a single bound.

nomiya
Cozy little Japanese-type pubs. Literally, "drinking shop."

Obon
See Bon.

o-chazuke
Rice gruel, a bowl of which is curiously soothing at the end of a long, hard evening of carousing.

o-chugen
The summer gift-giving season.

oden
A light stew of Japanese vegetables, etc.

o-hakamairi
The twice-annual occasion for the family to gather and visit together the family plot.

ohayo gozaimasu
"Good morning."

onigiri
A ball of rice with a pickled plum or piece of fish in the middle. Basic quick food.

"orai, orai"
Used to indicate to the driver of a bus or truck that it's OK to keep backing up. Presumably from the English "all right, all right."

o-seibo
The winter gift-giving season.

oshibori
A warm or chilled facecloth to refresh yourself with before taking tea, etc. One of Japan's little delights.

o-tsumami
Things to nibble on while drinking.

ringi system
Reputed to be an essential element of the Japanese system of management. Papers proposing various plans of action circulate through an organization. When all those concerned have signified their agreement by affixing their *hanko*, a plan is implemented, and rapidly, because everyone knows exactly how they fit into the scheme by the time consensus has been reached. Before that, behind the scenes, there is much informal discussion (called *nemawashi*) so that everyone is tuned in and thoroughly sounded out before they are called on to affix their hanko. The advantage is that unproductive public dissent is avoided, but the process can take a great deal of time.

romaji
The Roman alphabet.

Roppongi
The swinging, with-it, Western-exotic part of town, all rather a put-on, of course.

Saitama
The prefecture just to the north of Tokyo, considered by Tokyoites to be inhabited by bumpkins. *See also* Chiba.

"Saooo dake"

"Greeeen bamboo," the call of people selling long poles used to hang laundry out on.

Sensoji

Japan's most famous temple, in Asakusa.

sento

A public bath. Many sento are in wonderful old buildings with elaborately carved rafters and antique murals. They remain centers of community interaction in the older neighborhoods, but the new generation tend to consider them musty and old-fashioned.

shinkansen

The bullet train.

Shin Yokohama

New Yokohama Station, for the *shinkansen*.

shirankao

"Not-knowing face," the face someone puts on when they pretend not to notice something which you know damn well they do notice, as for example when they are sticking you in the ribs with a tennis racket on a crowded train but can't be bothered to make adjustments.

shitsurei shimasu

"Excuse me."

Shizuoka

Prefecture south of Tokyo famous for its tea.

shogatsu

The New Year's holidays.

shoji

Paper screen.

sumimasen

"I'm sorry."

takoyaki

Bits of broiled squid tentacles fried in batter balls. Classic late-night snack from a *yatai*.

tencho

Store manager.

"Tensei Jingo"

The daily light-touch editorial column in the *Asahi Shin-*

bun, translated and run a day or two later in the *Asahi Evening News* as "Vox Populi, Vox Dei." Ambassador Reischauer used to read "Tensei Jingo" first thing in the morning as a gauge of the public mood.

tonkatsu teishoku

The pork-cutlet blue plate special, an inexpensive lunch for the undiscriminating.

Tsukiji

A wonderful old part of town adjacent to the Ginza. Also, the informal name for the Metropolitan Central Market, the world's greatest fish market, because it's there.

Yamanote Line

The train line which runs in a circle around Tokyo's most expensive real estate, thus "inside" and "outside" the Yamanote loop is the most fundamental Tokyo geographical distinction.

yatai

A street cart selling light meals. The cheapest way to eat and, if you take the time to locate the best of them, not bad.

Yodobashi Camera

A very noisy retailer of cameras, watches, and gadgets near Shinjuku Station. Their loudspeakers harangue passersby in several languages at a volume which drowns out the traffic.

yukata

A light cotton summer kimono.

zokin

Cleaning rag. In Japanese schools, every class is responsible for keeping their classroom clean. One of the first things everyone learns is how to use their zokin in the prescribed way and how to wring it out properly. Consequently, all Japanese are convinced that no foreigner can ever know how to use a zokin the way it should be used.

zori

Rubber flip-flops.

ABOUT THE AUTHOR

Rick Kennedy was born in 1935 in Troy, New York, and educated at Princeton and Trinity College, Dublin. After an obligatory stint in the U.S. Army, he went to Europe where he was engaged by an Amsterdam import-export firm, which in 1962 dispatched him to Tokyo to set up a branch office. In Tokyo he submersed himself in the language and met his future wife, Mikie, who at the time spoke no English but wore a kimono with devastating grace.

Upon discovering that his main function in Tokyo was to express displeasure with Japanese manufacturers who had missed their deadlines, Kennedy decided to return with Mikie to New York, where for the next fifteen years he edited books.

When an old friend suggested there might be an opportunity for Kennedy to return to Tokyo as an advisor on editorial matters for Sony, he jumped at the chance. Kennedy has been at Sony since 1979, and in his meager spare time he writes columns for the *Japan Times*, the *Mainichi Daily News*, the *Tokyo Weekender*, and *The Magazine*.

Kennedy has two children, Ian and Mie, and lives with Mikie in Hiyoshi on the Toyoko Line. His hobby is contemplating the purchase of a folding kayak with which to explore Japan's lakes and rivers.